Training Your Puppy

THE ESSENTIAL GUIDE

Fiona Baird

Merlin Unwin Books

First published in Great Britain by Merlin Unwin Books, 2015

Merlin Unwin Books Ltd
Palmers House, 7 Corve Street
Ludlow, Shropshire SY8 1DB, U.K.
www.merlinunwin.co.uk

British Library Cataloguing-in-Publication Data:
A catalogue record for this book is available from the British Library

Designed and set in Calibri 11pt by Merlin Unwin
Printed by Leo Paper Products

ISBN 978 1 906122 82 9

CONTENTS

To Jean Lumsden

(Winner of the IGL Retriever Championship
with Field Trial Champion Treunair Cala)

This book is dedicated to my mother whose affinity with dogs and great love for them has fostered in me a certainty that life without a dog would be much poorer.

Without her experience, infinite patience and guidance over the years I would not have been in a position to write this guide which I hope you will find to be the secret to a happy family life with a well-trained dog.

Acknowledgements

Words cannot express the debt of thanks I owe to two people who worked tirelessly on my behalf to get this guide into a fit state to be shown to a publisher.

Peter Thomason turned my hand-written scrawl, with topics covered as I thought of them and in no particular order, into a well-presented manuscript.

Caroline Radula-Scott then did a wonderful job editing the guide whilst putting the contents into practice on her newly-acquired rescue puppy.

My thanks also to Bridget Wood who has been responsible for all the photogaphy. A perfectionist, she has gone the extra mile, literally, in pursuit of appropriate and stunning photos.

Karen and Merlin, the publishers, have been a joy to work with. Thank you both so much.

YOUR NEW PUPPY needs care, attention and training to prepare him for life as a member of your family.

This book will answer your questions and provide you with the help, guidance and information you need.

Follow these instructions and your puppy should develop into a delightful, obedient and devoted member of your family. He will bring you great companionship and happiness for many years to come.

Fiona Baird

1. CHOOSING YOUR PUPPY

Deciding to have a dog is a huge decision. It will affect your life and that of your family for up to 15 years. It is a commitment that should not be entered into lightly and if you are not prepared to give your dog adequate exercise once it has grown up, do not get a puppy.

WHICH BREED

Before deciding on which breed you want, ask yourself:

1. Does it have the right temperament?
2. What size of dog is suitable for you?
3. Is it suitable as a family pet?
4. Realistically how much exercise can you give it?
5. How much time are you prepared to spend grooming it?
6. Do you have suitable facilities in your house and garden to cater for the type of dog you want?
7. Is the breed you fancy generally biddable or is it likely to be difficult to train?

Points to remember:

1. Dogs that are known to need a lot of exercise will only be content and easy to live with if you give them as much as they need. Spaniels, for example, are bred to work all day. With plenty of exercise, structure and discipline, they are fantastic. So many people choose a spaniel because it is the 'right size, not too big and not too small and they look so nice'! However, I have lost count of the number of problem spaniels I have been asked to help with, usually because they won't come back. In every case, the owner has failed to instil discipline from the

outset and then compounded the problem by not giving the dog sufficient exercise. Be prepared to put in the work.

2. Don't fall into the trap of 'getting something a bit different'. Research the type of dog well. Why don't you see many of them around? There is a reason why the world sometimes seems to be populated solely with Labradors and Golden Retrievers – they generally have the perfect temperament with children. They are biddable, easy to train and loyal.

3. Terriers are usually very smart with huge personalities and are great fun but are you prepared to compromise with your terrier? Your word will never be law as it can be with many other breeds. Terriers often have a mind of their own together with wilful self-determination! If you live in the middle of a wood and your garden cannot be secured, a terrier is not for you.

4. Bearded Collies – are you really going to find the time to brush it thoroughly every day to stop that glorious coat becoming a tangled mess?

Nervous genes

I visited an eight-week-old Manchester Terrier, an uncommon breed, who had fear aggression. When the owners had gone to choose it, they were shown the mother who, safely behind a fence, was barking madly with hackles up. 'She is worried you might hurt her puppies,' they were told.

However, this little dog had to be re-homed before he was a year old. His fear aggression had become a danger to both his family and to visitors. It wasn't his fault and the owners had done everything right. Sadly, it was his genes that let him down. The owner reminded me in the course of this sad tale that at that very first visit, I had said that I thought there was real danger this puppy

more...

would bite someone. He was clearly a very nervous little dog.

The family now have a delightful Labrador, adored by them and all visitors. Don't be afraid to be sensible!

There are numerous books on the market that give valuable information on types of dogs, their personality traits and the ease with which you should be able to train them. A good one is *Encyclopaedia of Dog Breeds* by D. Caroline Coile, Ph.D.

STAGE 1: THE RIGHT LITTER

Having selected the right breed for your family, you now need to find the right litter. Word of mouth is best. Temperament is everything. You should be looking for:

- a puppy who will grow into a dog who can be trusted with children, whatever the provocation
- calmness
- biddability
- good looks, but only after the first three criteria have been met

Points to remember:

1. You should always see the bitch. If she is not available or the owners do not want you to see her, walk away!

2. It is unlikely you will see the sire. Serious breeders often drive hundreds of miles to use the right dog for their bitch.

3. Is the bitch calm and affectionate towards you?

4. Does the bitch glow with pride and enthusiasm that you have come to see her puppies?

5. Has the breeder asked you searching questions to establish whether you are suitable to have one of her puppies?

6. Are the puppies in a clean, safe environment with plenty of space?

7. Do the puppies look sleek, healthy and happy?

8. Are the puppies confident and out-going?

9. Have the puppies clearly had plenty of social contact with people?

10. Ask if the bitch and puppies have been wormed regularly and had treatment for fleas. (Puppies who have not been wormed will look underweight and at the same time will have bloated tummies.) If the entire litter are scratching incessantly, they have not been treated appropriately for fleas.

11. Does the breeder insist that the puppies stay with her until they are eight weeks old? A lot of breeders let puppies go at six weeks: they are at their most expensive to feed between six and eight weeks and it is a huge amount of hard work to keep them for the additional two weeks. However, the difference in their levels of maturity and confidence is huge if they remain with their siblings until eight weeks.

12. Does the breeder seem to know each puppy and its personality? Can she tell them apart easily?

If the answer to any of these questions is no, think very carefully before proceeding to the next stage.

Once you have located 'the right litter', then either a bitch or a dog puppy should have the right temperament and be equally straightforward to train. It is better to have the right puppy of either sex from the right litter than to have the sex you want from the wrong litter.

Dogs appear to have acquired a bad reputation as being liable to wander, to be harder to train, and to chase every bitch within miles! Yes they will do this, but only if you have acquired a dog puppy with the wrong temperament and then failed to exercise and train it properly.

Dogs are not subject to hormonal cycles as are bitches. Dogs are more akin to human boys. Girls tend to live life in shades of grey whereas dogs tend to live in a much more straightforward black and white world. Dogs also tend to be utterly loyal and, when properly trained, form an unshakeable bond with their owner.

Bitches are generally thought to be easier all round. A defiant bitch will almost certainly be easier to cope with than a defiant dog and a biddable bitch will probably be easier than a biddable dog. But with the right training, neither should be difficult.

Bitches give you the headache of three weeks, twice a year when they are in season and need to be kept away from the marauding male population! They tend to be physically smaller than dogs from the same breed. As with human girls and boys, bitches

will also tend to be gentler than their male counterparts. But again, basic temperament is the crucial factor in either dogs or bitches and a well-disciplined dog of either sex will be a delight.

STAGE 2: MAKING A CHOICE

Individual dogs will vary in their personalities just as people do. Some types and characters appeal more to us than others. Here are a few points you may wish to consider when selecting your puppy.

1. Take a good overview of the whole litter.

2. Look for any individual puppies that may be nervous but assess whether the puppy is really nervous or just timid and whether it may thrive when given a secure, structured and loving new home.

3. Do you want the 'me, me, me' puppy who rushes up to you? The children will fall for him as he has 'chosen' them. He will no doubt be bold and full of personality but he might not be as keen as some to follow the rules.

4. Don't forget to look for the puppy who is sitting back and sizing up the situation before he comes forward to join the inevitable throng. The saying 'Fools rush in' comes to mind. He will probably be both bright and biddable.

5. Then there are the other puppies, the ones who have not stood out for any particular reason in your first assessment of the litter. You can ask to take these ones, and any others you think you might like, away from the bulk of the litter where they can have a chance to show their potential.

6. Don't be afraid to take your time. Ask for puppies to be taken out of the litter or put back as many times as you need. A good breeder will let you play with a group or individual puppies while you search out the one who will become a valued, loyal member of your family for up to the next 15 years.

7. A breeder who is keen to find the right homes for her puppies will not mind you going more than once to ensure you make the right choice. If she gets to know you and she also knows all of the

puppies as individuals, she will be able to provide sound guidance to help you find the perfect puppy for you and your family.

8. Do not pick a puppy until the litter is at least five weeks old, preferably six weeks old. They take time to develop their individual personalities and the physical changes from birth to eight weeks are astounding.

The right puppy for your family

I gently laid a five-week-old German Wire-haired Pointer down on his back and with the palm of one hand, held him there. A Golden Retriever puppy's natural instinct at this point is to go floppy, back legs relaxed and akimbo: total submission. Not so the German Pointer. For 10 long minutes, he fought, he struggled and he tried to nip me before finally relaxing and getting the rewarding tummy rub that the Golden puppy would have earned immediately.

He wasn't an aggressive dog but he was a very dominant and belligerent dog. By the time he was nine months old, he had discovered that he could get his own way, first by growling and then, if necessary, by biting. He never ever tried to bite me but he did bite both his mistress and her 10-year-old son. He is now happily working on the Yorkshire moors with a man who knows all about Pointers. And the family? They are happy as well, with a bright, charming and biddable Golden Retriever bitch. Choose the right breed for you!

CHILDREN WHO ARE SCARED OF DOGS

If you have a child who is frightened of dogs, getting a puppy is a great idea. However, whether your child is apprehensive for no apparent reason or his fear stems from an unpleasant incident, it is crucial that you think carefully about the breed of dog to get for the perfect temperament: • calm but not nervous • bright but biddable

Small dogs, terriers in particular, tend to dart around in a manner that can be very unnerving to an anxious child. One child, who really did not want a dog as they scared her so much, told me she might be able to cope with a Golden Retriever. Fluffy, cuddly, loyal and dependable, it would have been the perfect answer. However, her family decided on a Border Terrier. Although a most delightful dog, living with the puppy and a frightened child proved a trial for everyone. The sheer speed and unpredictability of the puppy unnerved her.

Helping the child to make friends with a puppy:

- Don't try to force the child to like the puppy.

- Don't ask the child to touch the puppy.

- As far as possible, ignore both the child and the puppy and let them work things out between themselves.

- Don't shut the puppy away every time the child is in the room.

- Don't fall into the routine of doors opening and shutting while a shrieking child is kept away from the puppy.

- Of course you need to stop the puppy jumping up on the child or grabbing his or her clothes or hands but you will be teaching the puppy this anyway.

- Remember, it is not just the child who will be affected if you get this wrong. The puppy will also become as unnerved and frightened as the child if the situation is handled badly.

- Make it clear that while the child is free to ignore the puppy completely, both of them have to live in the same house and be in the same room when the occasion demands it.

- Unless the child is an only child, the puppy is likely to learn to ignore the fearful child quickly in favour of those who do want to play.

- There is nothing like telling children that they don't have to, or are not allowed to, do something to make them desperate to do it.

A terrified child

I once sold a puppy to a family with a child who was terrified of dogs. When they visited the litter, the parents kept telling the fearful child just to touch the puppy and to stand inside the whelping box and so on. But they should have said nothing and just let her watch her brother playing with the puppies.

At eight weeks they took their puppy home. At six months I rescued the puppy who was in a pitiable emotional state. He lay curled in a ball, too terrified to stretch out. He never came directly towards a door but always sneaked along the wall and then darted through. He was ever alert for any sudden loud human noise, his tail was always down and he looked permanently worried. In the car, he shook and dribbled throughout journeys.

Why? Because having failed to get the child to touch and interact with the puppy by forcing them together, the parents went to the other extreme. Doors had to be endlessly opened and closed to keep child and puppy apart. The dog was forever being manhandled to keep it away from the child who kept leaping on tables. The dog never knew when the next shriek was coming. On car journeys he shivered in the boot while the child shrieked in the back seat.

Within three weeks of being back with me, the puppy had regained his confidence and the strange patterns of behaviour were receding. The car was no longer a problem and his tail was wagging again. He was re-homed with another family with two children and, because of his fundamentally perfect temperament, he has been a much loved and valued member of his new family ever since.

2. PUPPY'S ARRIVAL

Having chosen your puppy, you will need to make some preparations and collect some basic equipment for his care before bringing him to his new home. Good planning will help him to settle in and will give you the confidence that comes from being properly prepared.

SECURING YOUR GARDEN

For your own peace of mind, it is important to check the garden boundaries for puppy-sized escape routes. Initially, escaping will be the last thing the puppy will want to do but as he gets bigger and bolder, a conveniently placed hole will be seen as an open invitation to explore further afield.

FREEDOM FENCING

If your property cannot be entirely fenced, freedom fencing may be the answer. An electric circuit is installed around your boundary and the dog wears a collar that automatically gives a small shock if he tries to cross the invisible 'fence' while it is switched on. This is different from the static electric collar which is controlled by the handler and should only be used as a last resort (*see page 125*).

If you train your puppy properly, he can easily be taught where the boundaries are without a visible barrier or a freedom fence. However, while you are in the process of training him, it is important that you should have the peace of mind afforded by a secure boundary.

A well-trained dog has no desire to get away from his owner. He relies on you and wants to be near you. Feed him and exercise him properly and take him out with you in the car whenever feasible. No dog wants to run away from a structured, stimulating, loving and fun environment. He might miss out!

An ill-disciplined, under-exercised dog whose meals arrive randomly and who never gets an outing, has very little to stay at home for.

SLEEPING ARRANGEMENTS

Decide whether you are going to use a cage or have a box as a bed. Either should be placed where the puppy will feel safe and secure and know he will be undisturbed. Buying a solid adult-sized bed at this stage is inadvisable, as it will make him feel insecure; the alternative is to keep replacing the bed as your puppy grows. Line the bed with Vet-bed, which is available from all pet shops and comes in different sizes. Most good breeders will have been using this in the whelping box for its warmth, ease of washing, and the grip it affords small puppies as they learn to get up on their feet. Vet-bed must be washed before using it for the first time.

CAGE OR BOX?

Cage: your puppy will grow fast so it will need careful thought to get a cage which is small enough initially for him to feel safe in but large enough to allow for growth without him becoming cramped. Ideally, two sides of the cage should stand against solid surfaces in order for your puppy to feel secure. You will need to make the cage cosy and comfortable to lie in with a suitable piece of Vet-bed or some soft alternative.

Box: A cardboard box with the front cut

away just enough to allow your puppy easy access while remaining secure and cosy makes a very good puppy bed. It provides a warm, safe place for him and has many other advantages:

- It is cheap.
- It can be changed as the puppy grows so that he will always be comfortable without being cramped or feeling lost in a space which is too big.
- If he chews, it is easily replaced.
- You can take the box in the car to help familiarise him with car journeys.
- It can provide a safe haven in any other house you visit with him while he is small.

LOCATION OF BED

There are several things to consider when deciding where to put the bed:

- Which room will the puppy be sleeping in at night?
- Puppies like to feel they are near you when they can be – you may need to select a day place as well as a night place for him to sleep.
- Where will you leave the puppy when you go out?
- If the puppy is continually shut away, he won't be able to discover his boundaries and what he will or will not be allowed to play with.
- Work out a strategy but be prepared to be flexible. Watch your puppy and he will no doubt sort out a spot for himself where he feels safe and to which he consistently retires. Is it possible to put the cage or box in this spot?
- Your puppy must be able to go to his bed or special corner and be left to sleep undisturbed until he is ready to wake

and play again. The discipline you are going to impose on him must be matched by clear rules for the children so they are aware of, and respect, the puppy's needs. When he wants 'time out' from playing, he must be left to sleep in peace. You would not wake a sleeping baby because you fancied playing with it, so neither should anyone be allowed to pester, harass, or generally annoy a sleeping puppy who needs sleep just as much as a baby does.

EQUIPMENT

Bowls: In pet shops, you will find excellent metal bowls for dogs with long ears like spaniels. These keep their ears out of the food. Otherwise, a flat-bottomed, plain metal bowl in an appropriate size will be light, unlike ceramics. They also come in a range of sizes and are easy to wash, unlike some plastic ones which hold water when draining whichever way up they are.

Any bowl is fine for water but bear in mind that your puppy must always have clean water available, particularly if he is fed on dried food. Make sure the bowl is large enough to hold sufficient water and sturdy enough that it can't be knocked over or chewed. There are very good plain heavy ceramic bowls available in all good pet shops which will meet these requirements.

Brushes: Initially, your puppy will need very little brushing but it is important to establish a good grooming routine while he is small. This will make him easier to handle once grooming becomes a necessity (*see page 44*).

Probably the best option for all long-haired breeds (e.g. Golden Retriever, Bearded Collie, spaniels and some terriers) is the 'In Style' Soft Brush for dogs. This will also be suitable while your puppy is small.

Once your long-haired dog has acquired its adult coat, a more comb-like brush will ensure no matted areas remain hidden in the feathering (long hair around hind quarters) or around the ears.

If you have a short-haired dog (e.g. Labrador, Border Terrier, etc), the first type of brush mentioned should be adequate on its own. For a smooth-haired dog (e.g. Weimaraner, Fox Terrier, Jack Russell, Dalmatian, Whippet, etc.), a grooming mitt or soft brush will be adequate.

Collars: It is a legal requirement that dogs should wear a collar but the legislation pre-dates micro-chipping. I would advise that all puppies should be micro-chipped as the best way to ensure their safe return in case of a mishap.

While I would not suggest that your dog breaks the law, there are two circumstances where I strongly suggest that the collar be removed for the purposes of training:

● In the house, collars provide great handles to use when trying to catch or grab your puppy but I must emphasise that you are never going to try to either catch or grab your puppy. The point of training is to get your puppy to do as you ask because you are in charge and he wants to please you, not because you are continually manhandling him with one hand firmly on his collar. If a puppy or dog is wearing a collar, you will find yourself holding on to it. Try it and see!

● On the lead. It is pointless using a light slip lead (*see page 16*) to aid training if the dog is also wearing a collar. He will not notice the slip lead, because with the weight of the collar, however light, he will never experience the feeling of comfort and freedom the slack lead affords. The collar can be replaced before you remove the slip lead once you are in a safe area for your puppy to run free.

Leads: A simple slip lead is the best. In effect, it is similar to a choke chain but I would never use a choke chain because the tightening chain, particularly in heavier versions, seems unnecessarily harsh. The weight remains evident to the dog even when it is not 'choking', unlike the light slip lead which will not be felt when loose. The slip lead is light to handle, not too thick, and supple.

The best ones are available in gunsmiths who stock the Turner Richards range of dog training equipment. Look for either the Sportsman's lead or the slightly more expensive Field Trial slip lead.

The slip lead is instrumental in training your puppy to walk to heel. The tightening effect helps to teach him the correct heel position. Once he has mastered it, he will barely feel the lead around his neck as it will be totally slack and so it will be easier to teach him to walk to heel off the lead later (*see pages 65, 66*

.

Extendable leads: Four reasons *not* to buy an extendable lead:

1. They are for the dog-owning population too frightened to let their dog off the lead. As you are following this guide, that immediately excludes you!

2. There is never an occasion when a puppy needs to have an extendable lead. They are at heel on a slip lead or running free. If you get the training right, you will be in control in both situations.

3. As you are teaching your puppy to walk to heel properly on a slip lead, the occasional use of an extendable lead would confuse him.

4. The first time you let the lead extend, you have just undone all of your good work on heel positioning with a slack lead.

TOYS

Do not be tempted by the large array of toys in pet shops, a lot of which encourage undesirable behaviour. Here is a list of readily available, cheap and useful toys which will keep your puppy entertained indefinitely:

Good toys

- Empty plastic bottles are great for rolling, crunching and carrying around.

- Old plastic plant pots – roll them, chew them, carry them, and toss them.

- Hide bones from the pet shop, or even better, good beef or lamb bones from the butcher. Any bone given to a dog must be raw, only cooked bones cause problems. Bones clean teeth, aid muscle development, provide hours of fun, and give necessary chewing activity, saving your home and furniture from damage.

- Tennis balls – but do not allow your puppy to become obsessed by them as this could turn the children's ball games into a nightmare.

Bad toys

Whatever balls you give your puppy as toys, beware of letting him get hold of ones that are too small and could be swallowed, e.g. ping-pong balls, golf balls, or squashy balls that could stick in his throat. **Other toys to avoid are:**

- Raggy toys designed for you to pull one end with the dog pulling the other. If you play this type of game, how can you expect your puppy to realise it is not a game when he has one of your best shoes, or a child's favourite teddy, in his mouth?

- Any soft toy or indeed any item which looks or feels like anything belonging to you or the children. Plenty of well-meaning children donate a teddy to the puppy only to have their favourite one, the one they can't sleep without, taken and chewed.

- An old shoe you don't mind being chewed. How is he going to differentiate between that and a new pair of Church's brogues?

- Shoe-shaped chews – the same applies, the puppy will have difficulty in learning not to chew other shoe-shaped items.

HAND-OVER CARE INFORMATION

You will need some information from the puppy's breeder to ensure proper continuity of care. Puppies, like small children, do not take easily to sudden changes in diet. As with children, it is also important to keep vaccinations and other important treatments up to date.

Your puppy's breeder should give you plenty of information on the type and quantity of food that your puppy is having and how often he should be fed. In many cases, it is likely that the breeder has chosen dried food. If you have decided to make a major change his diet then it sometimes has to be done gradually (take your vet's advice).

WORMING AND FLEA TREATMENT

All reputable breeders will have treated their litter for worms and fleas and should tell you when the next treatment is due. Your vet will provide you with all the information you need to ensure your dog's continued good health in this area. Discuss vaccination with your vet. Worming is particularly important in families with small children because dogs with worms may be carriers of toxicaris which can cause blindness. Infection occurs if a child gets dog excrement on their fingers and ingests it. The worm larvae can then travel through the body and cause severe damage to the eyes.

Puppies should be wormed at two, four, six, and eight weeks old. They should then be re-wormed every month until 6 months. Be careful about wormers and flea treatments bought from pet shops or supermarkets: reliable brands are only available from the vet. There is a 'spot-on' treatment that protects against fleas, lice, mites and lungworm. Lungworm is passed from snails and slugs to dogs and infects their heart and lungs and can be fatal, especially for puppies.

FIRST JOURNEY HOME

Now that you are fully prepared with basic equipment and the knowledge you need for your puppy's early care, the journey to his new home will be the first major change in his life. Puppies are trusting and will respond to comfort and calmness.

If there is more than one person collecting him, holding him gently on your lap is probably the most comforting. If you are on your own, an appropriately sized cardboard box with Vet-bed in the bottom

will make your puppy feel secure. Make sure you leave the box open, without a lid.

If you have decided to use a cage for your puppy's sleeping arrangements, this can be used instead of the cardboard box for the journey. Again, put a lining of Vet-bed in the bottom.

As soon as you arrive home with him, carry him from the car and place him on the ground in the garden. He will almost certainly stop for a pee. Praise him for this (see *pages 23, 24*) and then introduce him to his new home.

3. EARLY DAYS

During the first days with your new puppy, it is important to set the pattern for the more formalised training that will follow once he has settled into his new home. Your approach to him at this time is important and will help establish the foundation for obedience and a good relationship and enable you to gain full advantage from the guidance in the following chapters.

Your puppy's security and confidence comes from the guidelines and structure you give him. If you are worried and anxious, he will be too. You have to attain status as the 'leader of the pack'. The puppy comes below you, the children, and any other animals who were with you before he arrived. Always remember your puppy is a dog – not a toy or a child substitute. They don't think or behave like us, nor should they. However, in the same way as children, they do need structure, discipline and routine to be truly happy and secure.

GIVING YOUR PUPPY CONFIDENCE

To help him gain the confidence he needs to lead a happy life, with all behaviour issues and instructions you must mean what you say and stick to it. All members of the family must be consistent so that your new puppy will always know what is wanted of him and who is in charge.

Your tone of voice is everything and it takes time and confidence to gain the skills necessary to know when to be:

- encouraging
- pleased
- firm
- authoritative
- cross
- quiet
- cheery
- warm
- soothing

THE FIRST MEAL

Offer your puppy food as instructed by the breeder and initially try to keep to the feeding times he has been used to. Don't worry if he doesn't eat. Give him the bowl and plenty of time to decide if he wants it before removing it.

Try not to coax him and don't start feeding him by hand. Don't be tempted to try endless alternatives if he doesn't eat. If you are offering what he has been used to, he will eat when he feels ready. Some puppies get stuck in immediately and never look back. Some won't eat for 24 hours. Both are normal, as are the others who fall somewhere in-between. No puppy will starve himself to death, so continue to offer food, and then remove it if he is not yet feeling ready to start eating.

Don't leave food out for hours in the hope that he might eat a little at some point and don't offer food between the designated meal times.

As with everything else, start as you mean to go on. Establishing a clear routine for meal times is as important as every other aspect of training. As with the first pee when you arrive home, the first meals are also part of the training process.

THE FIRST NIGHT

If you are anxious about leaving your puppy alone on the first night, he will sense this and feel insecure.

Last thing before you go to bed, take your puppy out for a pee. Be jolly and praise him when he performs. Then be encouraging but matter-of-fact about going back into his bed/cage. Give him a cuddle and then leave him confidently with a cheery 'Good boy, see you in the morning'.

He may make no noise at all or he may howl incessantly. If you have handled him with confidence and encouragement on the journey to his new home and throughout his first day, it is unlikely that you will get anything worse than an intermittent cry. Do not go to him. While you may feel that he needs you, he is lonely, or that he needs reassurance, he must be left. By going to him you are taking the first step towards teaching him that making a noise gets him attention. He will have to learn to sleep on his own, so start the way you mean to go on.

By all means get up earlier than usual on his first morning. He will be thrilled to see you and lots of cuddles and praise are in order. You will have completed the worst night and as long as you didn't weaken, things will get better very quickly as he learns the routine and knows he can rely on you to reappear each morning.

HOUSE TRAINING

Only put newspaper down when you go out and at night as you don't want your puppy to get the idea that peeing or messing in the house is acceptable on a day-to-day basis.

Puppies need to be taken out for a pee when they wake up and regularly throughout the day. Decide on a word or phrase which the whole family will use consistently, e.g. 'Good boy. Out to do a pee now'. Then when in the garden, 'Do your pee'; and when he performs, 'Good boy to do your pee outside'.

When your puppy has the inevitable accident, take him to it and firmly say, 'What is this, NO, you do it outside'. He probably won't then do another pee outside but take him straight outside anyway for a short time. When the next pee is outside, be effusive in your praise.

Your puppy is likely to need to pee once overnight for a few weeks. Just ignore it but once you reach a stage when he is very reliable during the day, you can start using the same method of pointing it out as you did for the daytime training. All puppies are different and you may not have an overnight problem.

Be aware that it is very easy to be cross with bad behaviour and forget to reinforce the good positively, e.g. when you come down in the morning the first time the floor is dry, praise your puppy and again when he does his first pee of the day outside.

INTRODUCING YOUR PUPPY TO THE CAT

Puppies will naturally assume that your cat has been specifically provided to entertain him and if the poor cat turns tail and flees, then the puppy will need no further encouragement!

If the cat has a good right hook and is clearly prepared to stand his ground, ignore both the cat and the puppy and let the cat, who is the senior animal in the family, teach the puppy.

If, however, your cat clearly needs assistance, provide it. The cat was resident first and therefore to be respected. Gently restrain your puppy so that he can watch the cat but not chase. Say 'NO' and 'LEAVE IT' if the puppy tries to struggle free.

If the puppy does manage to chase or grab the cat, he must be swiftly removed by the scruff of the neck, as his mother would carry him, with a firm 'NO, LEAVE IT'. Generally, if everyone remains calm but alert to potential trouble, the situation will sort itself out and both puppy and cat will live peacefully together.

Playtime!

In my house were a nine-month-old Border Terrier puppy and a six-month-old kitten. A carpenter working in the sitting room called me, very worried because the dog was 'chasing' the kitten. 'Don't worry', I said, 'Just keep watching.' Sure enough, a minute later there were howls of laughter from the carpenter as the kitten launched himself off the back of the sofa and landed on the terrier, who leapt in the air with fright. A happy two weeks followed with the cat and the dog rolling around on the floor together, playing just like two puppies – or kittens!

INTRODUCING YOUR PUPPY TO AN OLDER DOG

Your older dog must be supported and helped by you as he adjusts to the new arrival. He will no doubt be thoroughly put out to start with and if the puppy is allowed to grab his tail and pull on his ears, life will become pretty miserable, particularly if he is too good-natured to object.

As with cats, if your dog is prepared to discipline the puppy, let him. At this point, a puppy is far more likely to listen to the warning growl of a dog than to you and it also serves to establish the pecking order. Clearly if there is any danger that the older dog might harm the puppy, then you must intervene.

You must also stop the puppy harassing an older dog who has had enough. Do not allow the puppy to get into the older dog's bed. Make sure the older dog has time and space away from the puppy. In time they may well share a sleeping space but be sure the older dog is happy with this arrangement first.

Most of all, as with the arrival of a new baby who has older siblings, make time for the older dog and give him plenty of attention. Let him do everything first.

LEARNING HIS NAME

If your voice is warm and encouraging and your arms are wide and welcoming and you are down at his level every time you call your puppy, he will quickly realise that the name you are calling relates to him. Reinforce this with 'Good boy' and his name every time he comes to you.

IN THE HOUSE

When your puppy gets hold of something you don't want him to have, do not chase after him. This instantly turns it into a game. While you may be able to catch your eight-week-old puppy, you certainly will not be able to catch your six-month-old puppy who has decided that this 'game' can be played at will, particularly at the end of a walk when he stays just out of reach waiting for you to either chase him or try to grab him to put on the lead.

If the eight-week-old has one of the children's toys, call him to you in a firm but encouraging voice. If he comes, great – get a gentle hold of the puppy on the top of his neck, behind his head and a gentle hold of the item. Say, 'DROP IT'. Don't be cross, just firm.

The hand on the neck allows you to stop him reversing away from you and turning it into a game of tug. When he lets go, tell him he is very good. Give him affection but don't over-excite him which may make him try to grab the offending item off you once more. If he does not come when you call, run away from him and then squat down with your arms open and inviting. No puppy can resist coming to you at this point and you are making the rules clear. You will never chase or grab at your puppy. He is going to learn to come to you willingly and enthusiastically.

SOFAS AND CHAIRS

Puppies and dogs who are allowed to get onto furniture are instantly elevating themselves to the level of the humans in the house. With the exception of dogs whose only problem is not coming back, every dog I have ever dealt with that had behavioural problems had been allowed at will on the sofas and chairs at home.

Small puppies, particularly those who will ultimately grow into large dogs, are hard to resist cuddling on your knee! You don't have to resist. Enjoy the cuddle but you say when the puppy can come up and when the cuddle is over. Don't wait for the puppy to decide it's time to wriggle off your lap. Place him firmly back on the floor before this happens. If you keep to these simple rules, your dog will not try to get up on the furniture as soon as your back is turned.

JUMPING UP

Through sheer enthusiasm and their desire for attention, all puppies will try to jump up on you. Start the way you mean to go on with a firm 'DOWN' as your puppy comes towards you. At the same time, have your hands with palms down and arms extended towards the floor. This gives both a vocal and a physical cue to the puppy. As the puppy is about to reach you, either bend or squat down where you will have better control and the puppy will not need to jump up.

If the puppy still manages to jump up, a tap on the nose accompanied by a verbal instruction to 'GET DOWN' should work. Make sure your puppy has all four feet on the ground before he gets the attention he desires. Once he gets the idea, you can also ignore him if he jumps up – keep your arms folded and avoid eye contact. Only when he stops, thinks and is quiet beside you should he get attention.

Children will be a harder nut to crack. Their tendency is to wave their arms in the air while saying, 'Get down. Get down.' This gives two completely opposing signals and you need to work on getting their hands down just as the adults do, as well as getting them down to the puppy's level. Older children with good balance can stick one leg up, knee towards the puppy, this makes jumping up more difficult.

GRABBING

All puppies will naturally try to grab or bite at your hands, sleeves and any tempting loose clothes. Children's shirt tails, skirts and trousers prove particularly irresistible. It is very important that children are taught not to pull away from the puppy. Apart from the obvious danger of torn clothes, you are again teaching your puppy that pulling and holding onto things is a good game.

Small children should stand still and call for help. Older children should be able to manage the following course of action themselves, particularly with a small puppy. If you put your thumb into the back of the puppy's jaw, there is a space with no teeth and

the jaw can be gently eased open. If necessary, hold on to the puppy with your other hand on the neck, behind the top of his head so that you can stop him pulling away as you release the jaw. Say, 'GOOD BOY' once he has released his grip, then gently put one hand round his entire jaw and say, 'NO GRABBING'.

There is a strong connection between puppies that are encouraged to play tugging games, as discussed below, and the ones who become obsessive about grabbing anything and everything. As in all things, you must be consistent. Repetition and consistency will win through!

With an older puppy where a persistent problem of grabbing has developed, you will find that applying a little gentle pressure on your puppy's foot has a magical quick release effect on his jaw. Remember to praise him when he lets go, even though he didn't mean to and is probably looking rather surprised. Clearly this is not a suitable strategy for children to use unless they are old enough and sensible enough to realise the potential harm they could do to the puppy's foot with misplaced but enthusiastic pressure.

PLAYING GAMES

Play is a very important part of a puppy's life. Through play, humans and all higher creatures learn skills and behaviours necessary for their physical and social survival. Young animals will play with older members of their group and with their siblings and other youngsters. Doing this they get exercise and stimulation, and they learn where limits may be set. As we are the leaders of the puppy's pack, it is important that the games we play teach him desirable behaviour and do not put him at risk.

BALL GAMES

- **Ball games** are generally good; tennis balls are the most appropriate. Beware of letting your puppy get hold of balls which are too small and could be swallowed, e.g. ping-pong balls, golf balls, etc. or larger squashy ones that when compressed could go down his throat.

- **Balls in the garden.** Playing football and other ball games can be good fun when the puppy is small but can develop into a problem when he is older and bigger. Unless the puppy learns to join the game only when invited and to stop when told, you may create an obsessive nightmare of a dog that constantly disrupts children's games and steals and punctures their balls. The puppy needs to be taught to obey the magic command, 'LEAVE IT'. To train him with balls, I suggest the following:

1. Put a football on the ground, say 'LEAVE IT'. When he ignores it, give lots of praise.

2. Gradually move the ball around more, still saying 'LEAVE IT' and giving praise when he does.

3. Supervise the first game of football. Let the children play but be with the puppy until he learns to get on and do his own thing and ignore the ball.

4. Playing retrieving games with a tennis ball is fine. If you are consistent, he will learn that football, croquet, golf chipping practice, etc., in the garden are to be ignored and that his games are with a tennis ball.

Bringing the ball back

Beware of falling into the 'He won't bring it back to me' trap. If you have been consistent in the house and nobody has chased the puppy, this will not be an issue. If however he thinks there is a chance of an added bit of fun because you might chase/grab him, he will come most of the way back and dance around daring you to chase or grab at him: ignore him completely and walk away. If he starts coming with the ball once more, be encouraging but until he is clearly happy to give you the ball on the 'DROP IT' command, keep ignoring him and walking away.

Stand still or walk away but never walk towards your puppy. This rule always applies in any situation where you need him to come to you or to give you an item. If necessary go back into the house and retrieve the ball later once the puppy has abandoned it. Your puppy will soon learn that games stop unless they are played by your rules.

There is an important difference between your puppy bringing things to you and chasing after you or the children. You should watch out for any games where the puppy may be encouraged to chase after people in an excited and uncontrolled way and then be rewarded by lots of cuddles or by escalating levels of excitement. Never allow the children to chase the puppy as, again, this will lead to problems in getting him willingly and consistently to come to you or bring items to you when you want him to.

Releasing and returning toys. When the puppy has his own toy, encourage him to come to you with it and when he is right beside you, encourage him to release it into your hand by telling him to 'DROP IT'. You can then be pleased and give it back to him. This balances all the times when he has given you items you didn't want him to have.

OTHER GAMES

• **Hide and seek.** Play this in the house or in the garden and when you start going out for walks. Start by hiding and then calling the puppy but then you must make sure he comes. This should result in the puppy having a greater awareness of where you are and the importance of keeping an eye on you in case you vanish.

• **Retrieving games.** As under 'Balls in the garden' (*see p30*) but if you have a puppy which you are going to train or have trained as a gun dog, do not throw any objects for him to retrieve, as you will be teaching your dog to 'run in'. Likewise, teaching the puppy to bring things to you is of vital importance in a budding gun dog.

• **Games under tables.** Many people seem to have trouble with puppies who discover that disappearing under a table, instead of coming when called, leads to a great game of chase which the owner can never win, running helplessly from one end to the other trying to 'catch' the puppy. This is again a direct result of falling into the 'catch him' trap rather than always making sure your puppy comes to you when you ask him to.

If this happens, you can either a) walk away, preferably out of the room and out of sight, and call the puppy once – if he comes, praise him. Or b) stay quiet and out of sight and he will most likely come to find you quickly because he is naturally curious, and as you failed to play the game, it lost its point. Alternatively, stay in the room and carry on doing anything you like but ignore the puppy. After a short while, you should be able to call him out. Once again, you declined to play the game so it is no longer fun for the puppy to stay under the table.

Always remember that once your puppy comes to you he should come all the way to you. Resist the temptation to grab him once he is within reach.

COMING WHEN CALLED

In all situations and locations, your puppy needs to learn to come when he is called. Much of the initial work will be in the home as I have described previously. With problems such as hiding under the table which can often occur at the same crucial times each day (e.g. when you want to put the puppy in his cage while you do the school run), allow more time. Call your puppy out with 10 minutes to spare and you will have time to use an appropriate strategy if he doesn't comply.

Outside situations

Your puppy will enjoy time to explore and play on his own or with children in the garden but he must learn that if you call him to come back into the house, he must come. Following on from the rule that you do not go to him, just open the back door and call his name in an encouraging voice which should aim to

Is he going to come?

sound as if it will be worthwhile for him to come. It will be, for when he arrives he will get lots of praise. If a meal is due and he hears encouraging noises from inside, it will be even more worthwhile and you will be reinforcing the benefits of good behaviour.

Once you see that he is definitely on the way back, leave the door open and move inside just out of sight. You can still use your voice to be encouraging. This should prevent the puppy from coming halfway towards you but not right inside because:

1. You are not standing in the doorway watching him. This would encourage the puppy to think it was OK to ignore you as he could see you weren't going anywhere without him.

2. While he cannot see you, there is no potential for a good game of nearly reaching the door and then racing off in the hope that you will either try to grab him or, even better, chase him.

Coming back inside: problem-solving

If you experience problems with getting your puppy to come into the house, try the following routine. However, it is essential that you leave plenty of time for this exercise. It will not work if you are desperate to get the puppy in before you have to rush out somewhere. And remember – no chasing and no grabbing and don't allow it to develop into a game.

1. Open the door and call him.

2. Walk inside, out of sight.

3. If he doesn't come, say nothing and shut the door.

4. Give him 10 minutes or so and repeat the exercise.

5. If all is silent, he will start to wonder what is going on. At this stage, if he comes to the door and barks, scratches, or whines: do not let him in.

6. Wait until he is quiet and then leave it just long enough for him to be able to associate his silence with reward and not with his making a noise. Open the door but say in a matter of fact way, 'IN YOU COME THEN'. Once inside praise him with a quick 'GOOD BOY'. Not giving him a lot of praise should show him he has done the right thing but he can't expect the praise he would have received had he come in straightaway.

If you have been meticulous from the start about following the always-get-the-puppy-to-come-to-you rule, you are unlikely to have any real problems in the garden. But, even the most amenable puppy will at some point try his luck to see if he really must come to you. This type of puppy is the one who is more likely to respond to direct confrontation. It will quickly become clear whether it is going to work or whether you need to take a more strategic approach.

Chasing your puppy to catch him...

Someone came to me with a nine-month-old Labrador who would not come to them when called. Sometimes she was a very long way away ignoring them completely and at others, she remained between 2 to 6 metres away, impervious to all attempts to get her back. The first time we went out for what was, in theory, a one-hour lesson, we got her back close beside us and relaxed three times in three hours! Six months of hard work followed during which the owners were relentless in following all the techniques I had taught them. It was worth it and the end result was a truly delightful and wonderfully behaved dog.

If only they had not started trying to catch her when she was small, a lot of anger, frustration and hard work could have been avoided.

TEACHING YOUR PUPPY TO SIT

Before you can get a response from your puppy, it is important that you have his full attention and concentration. Saying 'SIT' to a puppy that is bouncing around and clearly not listening to you is unlikely to prove successful. If your puppy is calm and close to you when you ask him to sit, that in itself will get his attention. **Eye contact is the real key**. If your puppy is sitting and looking intently up at you, it means you have got both his attention and concentration (*see page 62*).

Most people seem to find teaching their puppy to sit relatively easy. It appears to be instinctive to teach them early on. Once your puppy obeys this command, you will immediately have some control over him and a basis from which to continue training.

1. Always use a calm but authoritative voice when you give a command. Don't try to get a young puppy to sit in a room full of people when he will be distracted; nor when he is excited or leaping about.

2. When all is calm and quiet, place your hand, palm down, above the puppy's eye level so that he has to look up. As you say 'SIT', make a firm and positive downward movement with your hand. If he sits – fantastic! Praise him. If he does not, use your other hand to gently push his bottom down as you repeat the command. Praise him when he does sit, even if you had to push hard to place his bottom on the floor.

Caution: use commands sparingly

Once your puppy has learnt to sit, it's tempting to use it to show off your prowess as a dog trainer. This is understandable as you'll be pleased with your own and your puppy's progress. However, it is not a party trick but an important part of your puppy's education. You must therefore use the command (and all commands) wisely. Every time you find yourself about to tell your puppy to SIT, just ask yourself whether it is necessary. If it isn't, don't! Nothing leads to disobedience faster than a dog being endlessly asked to respond to unnecessary commands.

TEACHING YOUR PUPPY TO LIE DOWN

Teaching your puppy to lie down on command is very important as once your puppy lies down when told, you will find it much easier to form guidelines for when it is acceptable for him to be up and about and when he should be lying quietly. A dog that has never been made to lie down will probably spend a lot of time trailing round the house after his owner. This is not showing you how much he loves you. It is an example of the way a puppy or dog behaves when he lives life on his terms.

At eight weeks when you first bring your puppy home, it would be as inappropriate to be trying to force him to LIE DOWN as it would be to keep asking him to SIT. Young puppies, like children, have a short attention span, so don't expect too much.

An ideal way to introduce the concept of LIE DOWN is during the evening if you are going to have the puppy with you in the sitting room. He has, by then, had lots of fun, attention and food and should be quite happy to settle down for the evening. Give him a chance to wander around and find a place that he appears to like and then say 'LIE DOWN' firmly, but not crossly, and gently push him down. He will probably get straight up again but, with persistence, he will settle. Praise him but from the distance of your armchair or he will be up again.

This procedure establishes the pattern for peaceful evenings in the company of your puppy but on your terms and will also set a good foundation for later training to lie down (*see page 74*). Just be aware that while he is very young, when he wakes up, he will most likely need to be taken out for a pee.

Remember, you are in charge. If you want to play with your puppy at any stage during the evening, that is fine but it is you who instigates the fun and you who stops when you decide to. He must not be allowed to pester you until you give in.

Remember with all training...
- **KEEP IT SHORT**
- **KEEP IT FUN**
- **MAKE IT VARIED**
- **KEEP IT SIMPLE**
- **MAKE IT CLEAR**
- **MOST OF ALL – REMEMBER TO PRAISE**
- **MAKE SURE ALL INSTRUCTIONS ARE COMMANDS – NOT REQUESTS!**

TEACHING YOUR PUPPY NOT TO GO UPSTAIRS

You will have decided to which parts of the house your puppy will be allowed access. Many people choose not to allow dogs upstairs. If this is your decision too, make sure – as with every other part of his training – that the whole family agrees to the rules and will be consistent in applying them.

To teach your puppy that he is not allowed upstairs, say nothing until you get to the bottom of the stairs. Assuming the puppy has followed you, say 'WAIT' firmly as you start up the stairs. Watch him as you climb. The second he starts following you, go back down and push him gently down in front of you to the bottom again. Say 'WAIT THERE' and start up again.

Consistency and patience will be required to repeat this as often as it takes until you can walk to the top of the stairs with your puppy remaining at the bottom. Wait just a short time at the top where you can still see him. Then go back down again, pat him and praise him, 'You are a good boy to wait there'. Gradually, you will be able to stay upstairs longer and out of sight.

If your puppy appears at the top of the stairs once you have disappeared out of his sight, take him straight back down. Remember not to get into a chasing game or to try to catch him. If he is not going to follow you down easily, go and fetch his lead, get him to come to you, slip the lead on and take him downstairs. With a very young puppy, you should pick him up and carry him as negotiating stairs is not good for bone and joint formation at this age. Do not speak to him and particularly beware of telling him he is good and praising him for coming to you. He is good for coming to you but that is not the issue. He was naughty to have come upstairs in the first place, so a very matter-of-fact silence is in order until you reach the bottom of the stairs, slip off the lead if you had to resort to using one, and repeat 'WAIT THERE' before going back upstairs once again.

LEAVING YOUR PUPPY

If you get worried and anxious every time you leave your puppy at home alone, he will immediately assume there is something to be worried about. But if you start very early on leaving your puppy for short periods at first, with a cheery 'Good boy, see you later', he should assume all is well and settle down to sleep (*see Common Problems page 104*).

VISITING THE VET

So often one hears, 'My dog hates going to the vet'. This does not have to be the case, as my dogs adore visiting the vet and are most put out when it is not their turn!

This is due to a number of reasons:

- Because I am the leader of the pack, they trust me to do the best for them.
- I have become the leader of the pack through giving them clear rules and boundaries within which to live.
- I am consistent in my response to any given situation.
- I praise all good behaviour and either ignore or reprimand bad behaviour.
- Most of all, I mean what I say so once I ask something of a dog, I will see it through, no matter how long it takes or how much it tries my patience.
- My body language and voice always exude confidence so that the dog will do as I ask and know there is nothing to worry about.

The result is that when I walk into the vet's surgery with a dog, my assumption is that he is thinking, 'Yippee! A fun trip out'. If the vet should then have to do anything unpleasant, I remain calm and say gently, 'Good boy, keep still'. My hold on the dog is firm but one hand will be giving a reassuring stroke. Once it is over, I praise him.

FEEDING AND DIET

Whatever type of diet you are planning for your puppy, it is important to feed him the correct amount for his size and age. They are all different, just as we are, so following the feeding guide on the back of the pack is just a starting point. A growing puppy will need the quantity increased as he grows and your best guide is to be aware of how your puppy looks on an almost daily basis.

Dogs and puppies should have a 'waist' – a defined indentation just forward of their hind quarters. A 'pinched' look, however, suggests they are underweight. You should be able to feel their ribs easily but there should be a healthy fleshy feel between your fingers and their ribs. You should be able to feel their spine without having to press hard to find it, which immediately suggests a fat dog. However, neither should a light touch make you aware of each joint of their spine. If you look down on your puppy or dog and there is a straight square look from front to back, he is likely to be overweight.

A dietary tale...

A very thin Golden Retriever bitch, aged six months, arrived for training. She was so thin I was incapable of hiding my horror. She stayed with me for four weeks. By starting her with five small meals a day and then by gradually increasing the amount of each meal and reducing the number of meals gradually back to the appropriate two, I succeeded in her gaining 5.5 kilos! She looked wonderful and her thrilled owners could not believe she was the same dog.

What was their mistake? They had read the breeder's advice on a suitable quantity of food for an eight-week-old puppy and never thought to increase it as she grew.

Take vet's advice on your puppy's diet

Once you have had your puppy for a while and got to know him better, you will begin to be more aware of the signals he is giving you about food and meal times.

Whilst you should stick to the diet used by the breeder to start with, do take your vet's advice on a suitable alternative if you feel that your puppy could benefit from a different diet.

Sadly there are breeders who will feed puppies on the cheapest brands of food to save money. You really do get what you pay for!

Lack of appetite

If your puppy is not eating well, there could be a number of reasons for this. Perhaps he really does not like what you are giving him so if you have tried putting food down and taking it away, as described on page 22, and he is still not eating, do try an alternative food.

- Is the puppy being fed in a peaceful environment so that he can concentrate on eating or are the children running around shrieking while he is expected to eat his food in the middle of the kitchen floor?

- Are you spacing meals evenly through the day? An 8-week-old puppy will need four meals a day which will reduce in the first few weeks to three meals and finally down to two meals a day by the time he is about 6 months old.

It may be that you are feeding four times a day and actually your puppy is ready to drop to three meals and will instantly eat better as a result.

Permanently hungry puppy

Some puppies appear to be constantly starving.

- An inferior brand of food might be the cause so splash out and buy good quality food. Would you feed your children cheap burgers and chips every meal or do they get wholesome food?

- Are you remembering to stick to the worming regime that your vet will have suggested when you had your puppy's inoculations done? A wormy puppy may well be a very hungry puppy.

- Some dogs are greedy, some are picky, most are no problem at all but there just might be a medical problem as to why your puppy is not eating, so trust your instinct and consult the vet if you need to.

The good health of your puppy and on through adulthood depends on your attention to his diet. An underweight puppy will struggle to grow and develop healthy bones and muscle if he is not getting the necessary level of nutrition. An overweight puppy is likely to become an obese dog, creating an unnecessary strain on his joints, heart and circulatory system. He will also develop foul-smelling breath and be prone to gum disease if his teeth are dirty.

It is a myth that all old dogs have bad breath. It is important that you clean your dog's teeth regularly. There are a number of products available and your vet can give you advice on these. Chewing raw bones helps in the development of muscles and provides stimulation and enjoyment and keeps your dog's teeth and gums healthy. Comments are often made that my 13-year-old Golden Retriever never seems to have bad breath. This is always said with surprise. The answer is that I took a lot of trouble to ensure that her teeth were kept clean and she did love being out in the garden chewing on an occasional raw meaty bone from the butcher.

Never ever, give your dog cooked bones. It is these that have the risk of sharp chips breaking off and causing internal damage.

Synthetic hide bones, pig's ears, and all the other similar delicacies sold in pet shops do not have the same benefits as raw bones. Your puppy will love them and they will do no harm but beware, the majority are laden with calories so you should adjust your puppy's meal accordingly on a day when he has these treats.

HOW TO GROOM YOUR PUPPY

It is important to establish a consistent grooming routine that is acceptable to your puppy. All puppies leap around, try to grab the brush, roll over when you want them standing up, try to get up when you want them lying down, and generally think it is a great game. You must be firm. A tap on the nose accompanied by 'LEAVE IT' each time he tries to grab the brush should get the message across.

Start with your puppy standing up. Use the command 'STAND STILL' and then make sure that he does. This will take persistence, patience and consistency but it will be a lot easier than allowing him to get away with playing up now than having to cope with a boisterous six-month-old later! Praise him when he does stand still and make these initial sessions very short. He will soon get the idea that the better behaved he is, the quicker it will be over. Once puppies start to relax, they also begin to realise that being groomed is a pleasurable experience.

When you have made your puppy stand still and given him a quick once over, it is time to get him to 'LIE DOWN'. This should be right on his back and you must make sure he stays like that until he relaxes completely, even if to start with, no brushing takes place.

Puppies instinctively realise this position is one of total submission. To indicate their lower position, the alpha male in a pack would pin down the young upstarts until they submitted. This

is therefore a great way to reinforce your position as the alpha male of your 'pack'.

Some puppies will instantly be very happy to roll over, have a quick brush and then a good tummy tickle as a reward before they get up. Others will struggle and fight you all the way so it is particularly important with the less naturally submissive type that you stick to your guns and persist until they submit. (How easily your puppy submits will be a good indicator for how easy he will be to train.)

There are observable differences between a puppy that relaxes into a submissive acceptance and one that remains tense and still on sufferance. Pay particular attention to muscle tone: you will feel if the puppy is relaxed and floppy or tense and ready to jump up. Relaxed puppies have floppy legs that they will allow you to move around. Tense puppies will retain stiffness and energy in their legs, as if waiting to push you away or to stand up. Only when your puppy truly submits should he get the reward of a tummy tickle. If you get him to relax by tickling his tummy, he is not submitting: 'I will only lie on my back if you tickle my tummy' is very different from 'I am lying down because if I am very good, I may get my tummy tickled as a reward'.

45

What your puppy learns from being groomed

Grooming is not just something you should do for the physical welfare of your puppy, it is also a valuable training aid:

- STAND STILL is a very useful command when you want to hose down a muddy dog at the end of a walk and then dry it.

- LIE DOWN is another important command for a dog to understand, so that you can tell him to lie down out of the way during your meal times, in the evening when you want peace and quiet, in the car, or when you are visiting friends' houses with him, or simply when he is making a nuisance of himself.

- TOTAL SUBMISSION. Remember that in order for your puppy to be able to submit, he must feel safe to do so. That, along with your demands as pack leader, reassures him that you will always ensure his safety and well-being.

- LEAVE IT. Once he realises you mean 'Don't try to grab either the brush or the hand that holds the brush', he should be able to transfer the understanding of the command to other situations, e.g. when you see him about to grab an abandoned shoe.

Washing

I am often asked whether you should shampoo your dog. The answer is an emphatic *no* unless:

- You have been prescribed the shampoo by a vet to treat a specific condition.

- Your dog has rolled in something unspeakable and even then I suggest you shampoo only the affected area.

Your dog's coat has been designed by nature to keep him warm and allow him to dry quickly. If you shampoo your puppy regularly, or even occasionally, you are likely to upset the natural balances of his coat.

A dirty or muddy puppy at the end of a walk is easily dealt with by using a hose pipe, cold water (regardless of weather), and a good rub down with a clean towel. Dogs do not feel cold in the same way as we would under a cold shower. While they may take a while to get used to this routine, it will not harm them and in summer they will positively enjoy it. In reality, it

is usually only the legs, feathering and undercarriage that need a good flushing and they do love the warming rub afterwards.

ADVICE ON EXERCISE

It is vital that you do not over-exercise your puppy. The right amount of exercise provides fun, stimulation and an introduction to the world outside your home. A 10-15 minute stroll is quite enough for a 12 to 16-week-old puppy. The worst form of exercise is on a lead walking on a pavement at your natural speed. Too much exercise too soon, and the wrong sort of exercise, may damage a puppy's developing bones and joints. If you do not live within two or three minutes of a field or park, either carry the puppy there or take him in the car.

A puppy that flops down on a walk has had enough. Pick him up and carry him home. If you get it right, he will still be full of beans at the end of the walk but very happy to have a long sleep once he gets home.

4. BASIC PUPPY PSYCHOLOGY

DOGS ARE NOT HUMAN

Dogs are pack animals and all packs must have a leader. When people have serious problems with their dogs, almost without exception, it is because the dog has become the leader of the pack.

You must be the leader of the pack, providing consistent rules and discipline. The pack, in this instance, is your family and other pets, as well as the puppy. People worry that if they discipline their puppy too much, the puppy won't love them. Your puppy will love you more than you can imagine once it is leading a structured and disciplined life: you will form a bond and trust in one another, which should lead to a happy, secure and contented life together.

Dogs who find themselves elevated to the position of pack leader are the ones who whine, bark and scratch at doors when you leave them alone. Why? Because they feel responsible and worry about you.

Importance of being leader of the pack...

A bitch puppy of a large and unusual breed was 16 weeks old when I first met her. By this time she had already bitten the gardener and one of the adults in the family. In trying to assess this puppy, I too got bitten; not badly and never again but the incident alerted me to the potential danger to the children in the family.

As this was a breed I didn't know, we sought advice from breeders of this type of dog on how to handle the situation. We were told 'Be brutal! You will have to pick her up off the ground and shake her and really show her who is the boss.' *more...*

I was horrified. This went against every instinct I had for dealing with a puppy of this age. Equally, I could see that unless we could persuade this puppy that she was not the leader of the pack and get her to submit, she would not be safe enough to stay with the family. A lot of hard work followed until, at last, the dog would even allow the three-year-old child to take her food away. The breeder had said, 'If you do this and get it right, she will become an utterly loyal, safe and loving member of the family,' and she has.

She was not an aggressive bitch, just genetically very dominant. I later learned that the breeder had also said that he would not sell the family a dog puppy, only a bitch! This is an extreme case but it serves to stress the importance of having your leadership accepted.

DOGS *DO* UNDERSTAND ENGLISH

It is extraordinary how much of our language dogs can understand. A lot of this comprehension arises from the tone of your voice as much as what you actually say, so think about how you speak to your puppy. If you sound cross when you give an order, your puppy will be anxious and unlikely to do as you ask for fear of doing the wrong thing. A firm, low voice that gives a clear message that you expect to be obeyed is crucial. Once your puppy has mastered a skill and then decides not to obey while looking at you defiantly as you give an order: e.g. 'SIT', you will need to add extra feeling to your voice: 'I SAID SIT, DO AS YOU ARE TOLD, AT ONCE!'

PRAISE

As in all aspects of training, do praise your puppy when he does as you ask. This applies even after saying 'SIT' three times and you have had to resort to pushing his bottom onto the ground with your hand.

RESPECT FOR YOUR DOG

Dogs have feelings, just as we do. They feel pleasure, fear, anxiety, excitement, etc. They also have 'off days' when they are under the weather or possibly ill. Be aware of your puppy's feelings. It will take time to get to know him, just as we take time to get to know each other. Like us, they are all different: some are very bright and others are really rather stupid. Is your puppy not doing as you ask because he doesn't understand or because he is being defiant?

A sensitive or nervous puppy will need lots of encouragement and praise to reassure him that all is well and he is doing the right thing: shouting or smacking a puppy that you perceive as being defiant but is in fact terrified of doing the wrong thing will only make matters worse. On the other hand, being too sweet and feeble with a bold, bright and defiant puppy will never see you elevated to the position of pack leader.

Excitable puppies will need calm, soothing praise or you will end up with mayhem every time he does something right, whereas a timid or nervous puppy will need enthusiastic praise so that he is in no doubt how pleased you are.

These examples are just a guide. It is impossible to cover every situation that may arise with different personality types but they should illustrate the importance of respecting your puppy and help you to put the appropriate care and thought into how to get the best from your puppy as you train him.

You and your puppy have a long road ahead with plenty for you both to learn but it is worth taking time, putting in the effort, being consistent and establishing a solid framework within which you, your family and the puppy will all enjoy each other. Owning a dog should be fun and rewarding. If you give him what he needs, he will reward you with years of love and devotion in return.

HOW PUPPIES LEARN

The better a puppy is trained, the stronger the bond will become between dog and owner. It is no accident that highly trained working dogs are never far from their owners; the working relationship can become almost telepathic. The handler is still the leader but dog and owner/handler have become a team with the handler as team captain. They trust each other. The dog shows initiative when required but also follows orders and guidance in pursuit of a common goal.

Puppies learn through repeated clear instruction and consistency. They must be praised for getting things right and reprimanded for bad behaviour. Tone of voice and body language is crucial as dogs are acutely aware of our moods.

A sensitive terrier

An extreme example of sensitivity was demonstrated by a terrier that lived with me for six months, having been rescued from his alcoholic owner. She loved him but had no control over her life and this sensitive, bright little dog suffered serious emotional damage caused by constantly worrying about his inconsistent mistress.

One day, after he had been with me for about three months, something made me cry; watching the person cry who had given him back his life, proved too much for him. He crumpled before me, shaking and distressed. It took much reassurance for him to regain his composure and to wag his tail once more.

In that moment, when I had started to cry, he was transported back to life with his previous owner who had sobbed uncontrollably for much of the time. We should never underestimate how much our behaviour can affect our dogs, sometimes having a long-term impact.

This awareness is apparent in many situations and becomes more acute the closer you are to your dog. This closeness and bond comes through training. An untrained, ill-disciplined dog is unlikely to show any sensitivity to your mood as he is entirely independent and 'out for himself'. However, a dog that has truly bonded with you will stay close with his head on your knee when he senses you are unhappy or brooding.

CREATING PROBLEMS

While good behaviour is learned through repetition, bad behaviour can be learned from our inadvertent or inconsistent cues and reinforcement. Without realising, you could be training your dog to do something that becomes a real problem. Most common, is the dog that does not come back to you (*see pages 113-116*).

How do problems of this nature start? Possibly your eight-week-old puppy got hold of one of the children's toys. Everyone chased him, caught him and retrieved the toy. Job done? No, because the next time you called him to you, he did not come. No problem – go and catch him! Your puppy realises this could be a good game and you find yourself constantly trying to catch him as he races around the furniture and under tables.

When you start taking your puppy for walks, you call him to you but he is having a good time sniffing and playing. This is not a major problem as he is small enough for you to be able to catch him but you will not be able to do this when he is six months old. He will then probably become a dog who seldom returns when told. He has learned that this game can be played at will: when you call him from the garden, when you want him to get into the car, when you want to put him on the lead at the end of a walk, and definitely when he has something in his mouth which he knows you want!

PATIENCE, PERSISTENCE AND CONSISTENCY

The moral of the story is that it's never too early to start establishing good patterns of behaviour. Of course, it will be hard work and a puppy with any personality will test even the best trainer but patience, persistence and consistency will win through and the result will be a pet who is welcomed by friends, can be walked by anyone, and is a delight to have as part of the family.

REWARDS

Should you use treats as a reward for good behaviour? Using treats is an established method of training and, if it works for you, that's fine. I wouldn't discourage anything that works in dog training. However, it poses the questions:

- When do you stop using treats?
- When will the dog start doing what you ask because it has to?
- Has the reward become a bribe?
- When will the dog start doing what you ask because it wishes to please you, rather than because there is something in it for him?

Treats are also tit-bits which if fed endlessly will produce a fat and unhealthy dog. Endless treats also inevitably lead to incessant begging.

I have never used food as a reward, preferring to have dogs do as I ask because they want to please me. When they get things right, my praise is lavish. When they disobey, my tone of voice says it all. Generally, unless you are unlucky, dog breeds that are suitable as family pets have a fundamental desire to please and they flourish in a consistent regime that gives them clear rules and boundaries.

BEING FIRM

Think of it as if your dog lives in a square with a solid black line around it. All good behaviour is within the square and while your dog conforms and follows the rules, there is plenty of freedom, fun, and praise. If your dog steps outside the line, you must be quick to reprimand. Once again, tone of voice is crucial: 'NO!' said very firmly with its meaning clear, will work wonders.

For added force with a persistent offender or offence, get your puppy by the scruff either side of the neck, hold firmly, and lift his front feet just off the ground. Then say, 'I SAID NO' looking him straight in the eyes.

BEING CONSISTENT

Remember the black line is a solid one. It should not have a wiggle here or there for the days you do not really feel like following an instruction through to a satisfactory conclusion. Nor does it have to have a convenient gap for the dog to escape metaphorically when you can't be bothered to pick up on something that you know is wrong and has been an issue in the past.

COMMANDS

Most eventualities can be met with the following commands:

1. ***DON'T YOU DARE!*** is a phrase to use before anything else as you see your puppy about to grab, jump, etc.

2. ***LEAVE IT***

3. ***GET DOWN*** – used to stop your puppy jumping up

4. ***WAIT***

5. ***NO***

6. You are a ***GOOD BOY*** – repeat as often as needed

7. ***DROP IT***

8. ***SIT***

9. ***LIE DOWN*** – very useful when the puppy constantly follows you around the house.

TIMING

DON'T YOU DARE! and LEAVE IT are excellent commands to use. For example, you see that your puppy is about to pick up a shoe lying on the floor. Don't wait for it to happen. Get in first with 'DON'T YOU DARE!' followed by 'LEAVE IT' if the puppy keeps advancing to the shoe. He will know exactly what you are talking about and, no doubt, he will be very impressed with your powers of perception. Do this a few times and he will stop bothering to try to get the shoe, knowing that you know what he is thinking!

If the puppy does pick up the shoe, remember – he must bring it to you and release it on the command 'DROP IT'. If you sound cross, or shout, he will probably hang on tighter, so be calm and use a soothing voice. Once he has let go, put it back on the floor, saying 'LEAVE IT' as you do. Once he has the message and ignores the item, praise him with 'Good boy to leave it'.

This strategy can be used for many of the situations which tend to be a normal occurrence in most households with a puppy:

- Picking up items you don't want him to have (as in the example above)
- Taking things out of the dirty washing basket
- Taking clothes out of the clean washing basket while you are trying to hang them on the line
- Stealing the children's toys, either from the floor or the toy box
- Taking things out of waste paper bins

PLAY AND STIMULATION

Puppies need a balance between fun and rest. It is important to be aware that some games can be helpful and positive in developing good habits and obedience but others can give the wrong message and either confuse or teach the wrong behaviour. It is also important to understand that puppies need frequent rest and will get tired and you should be alert for the puppy that is exhausted and trying to get away from over-enthusiastic children who are unaware that he is trying to get back to his safe spot to sleep.

VERY YOUNG CHILDREN AND PUPPIES

Do not let very small children pick up the puppy. It is hard enough for an adult to maintain a firm hold on a wriggling puppy. Being dropped by a child will at best put a strain on developing joints and at worst could lead to serious injury. Get your children into the habit of sitting on the floor to cuddle the puppy. This has the added advantage that the puppy will not be trying to jump up at them.

So many people say to me 'But I can't stop the children...' my answer is always the same: 'Who is in charge?' Your puppy has no way of defending himself from over-enthusiastic children who will need to learn that some of the things they are doing to him could cause injury.

You are the only protection your puppy has. Do not let him down. This reliance on you is also an important part of the bond that should form between the two of you as you establish the rules and structure within which he will live. He needs to trust that you will protect him.

Both children and puppy learn respect for each other through establishing rules and guidelines for when they are playing. Children generally respond well when they realise that the puppy is, at least initially, more vulnerable than they are. They gain a sense of responsibility, caring and control through helping to look after and play sensibly with the puppy.

BEWARE OF GIVING MIXED MESSAGES

Jumping up is a classic scenario with children. Children tend to wave their arms in the air to get them out of reach of a puppy who might be trying to grab their hands and sleeves. While doing this they are very sensibly saying, 'Get down. Get down!' The verbal command to get down will be ignored by the puppy that is mesmerised by the arms that are suggesting something completely opposite.

As the puppy comes towards them, if they are standing up, get your children to keep their arms down, palms towards the floor. The verbal command to GET DOWN will be strongly reinforced by the physical action.

Children can also be encouraged to kneel down with their arms wide so the puppy has no need to jump up and the child is then in a far more secure position to handle the puppy's natural exuberance and affection.

Children who endlessly call the puppy's name while playing with him give another mixed message: they don't usually want the puppy to come to them but they are inadvertently giving him a strong message that he can ignore his name when called. You must be very careful to be consistent so that every time you or anyone else calls the puppy's name, he is in no doubt that it is because you need him back to you as quickly as possible.

THE NEED FOR CONSISTENCY WITHIN THE FAMILY

Where care of the puppy is concerned, it's very important that the whole family agrees and then keeps to a plan. You must all agree:

- on the commands you will use
- in which rooms the puppy will be allowed
- the puppy will not be allowed to jump up
- biting and grabbing at hands and clothes is unacceptable
- no one will chase and try to catch the puppy
- the puppy will learn to come to you when called.

MEETING NEW PEOPLE

It is very good for your puppy to meet lots of new people. He will learn to be confident with strangers but equally important, he will discover that all the same rules apply no matter where or with whom he is. Whenever possible take your puppy with you to visit friends and family so that he learns to adapt to different situations in a calm and controlled manner. With persistence, patience and consistency, you will be able to expect the same high standards of behaviour whether you are at home or somewhere new.

Dogs who do as they are told, remain calm, don't jump up, and lie down quietly when the situation demands are almost universally welcomed. Dogs who are out of control are unlikely to be welcomed back after the first visit. We are all familiar with the charming couple with children who are so ghastly and ill-disciplined that we dread them coming round for lunch. Do you want to become that family because of your dog?

TRAINING FAMILY AND FRIENDS

It is very important that you do not let your friends and family, who all think your new puppy is the cutest thing ever, destroy in a moment all the good work you are doing. Unlike your own children, who will have already learnt about mixed messages, the importance of not saying one thing while their actions suggest something else must also be indicated to others.

PATIENCE, PERSISTENCE AND CONSISTENCY

Finally, if as a family you remain patient, persistent and consistent from day one, the training process should prove both fun and rewarding from the start.

5. FIRST STEPS IN TRAINING

This chapter will assist you in forming a bond with your puppy, instilling obedience and avoiding mistakes in the early stages.

REMEMBER

Patience, persistence and consistency
are the keys to successful training.

Formal training starts the first time you take
your puppy for a walk.

Your puppy must have completed his course of
inoculations before you take him out.

Once you decide on a course of action or give an
instruction, you must see it through

Every time you give in and the puppy is allowed to do
something his way, he will be encouraged to defy you again and
again until you take consistent action.
Then he will realise there is no point in ignoring or
disobeying you, as you will always win in the end.

The key remains: patience, persistence and consistency

IN ALL TRAINING...

- KEEP IT SHORT
- KEEP IT FUN
- MAKE IT VARIED
- KEEP IT SIMPLE
- MAKE IT CLEAR
- MOST OF ALL – REMEMBER TO PRAISE

COMMANDING ATTENTION

Before you can get a response from your puppy, you have to have his full attention and concentration. Saying SIT to a puppy who is bouncing around and clearly not listening to you is unlikely to prove successful. If your puppy is calm and close to you when you ask him to sit, you will have more chance of gaining his attention.

Eye contact

Eye contact is the real key. It should be established as early as possible. A quick glance does not count. Your puppy needs to learn to look up at you intently; in effect, asking your permission to go on to the next thing. It emphasises your position as the person in charge. If your puppy has sat and is looking intently up at you, it means you have both his attention and his concentration. Then, and only then, can you move on to the next command. Once you establish good eye contact, you will find that your puppy looks at you more intently in many different situations.

Eye contact at meal times

One very good way of establishing the pattern of obtaining eye contact is at feeding times. Most people seem to be aware that getting a puppy to wait before he has his food establishes good manners. This usually entails the food being on the floor with the puppy staring at it in desperation. Use this to gain eye contact. Place the bowl on the floor then stand between your puppy and the bowl. Tell your puppy to wait and then wait for him to look up to you in a questioning manner; in effect, asking, 'Hey, why aren't you telling me I can eat?' Immediately, tell him that he is a good boy and that now, he can indeed eat his food.

Be careful to remain in control of the situation so that if and when he gets bored with waiting and before he realises that looking at you and asking your permission is the key, you can whisk the bowl away to stop him diving in and eating the food anyway.

Once your puppy has mastered the rule of eye contact before being given permission to do something, do not continue to use his meal times as a training aid. While he should not dive into his bowl, almost knocking it out of your hand, he should also not be kept waiting unnecessarily while you congratulate yourself on your 'control' over him. A client once told me with great pride that he could walk around the house and back, leaving his dog waiting patiently by his food bowl. This is not leadership; it is domination, which also has an element of teasing.

At the beginning of a walk

Eye contact as a means of gaining your puppy's attention is very important at the start of every walk but shouldn't be attempted until he is 12 weeks old and happy on the lead (*see First Walk on page 65*). Once you have your puppy sitting quietly, calmly and still, slip the lead on and say nothing. Some puppies, by now, will instinctively and immediately look up at you with a penetrating gaze: this is perfect. Do not lose the moment, immediately say, 'GOOD BOY' followed by the next instruction which will be 'HEEL'.

Do not ask your puppy to look at you and do not use his name. If he remains sitting quietly and still but is looking everywhere but at you, try moving your legs around so that they block his view. If he then looks up, immediately say, calmly and quietly, 'GOOD BOY, HEEL' and walk off slowly. Your puppy will not learn to walk to heel properly on a slack lead if you race off at the speed you think he would like best.

When extra efforts are needed to gain eye contact, be careful not to stand so close to your puppy that he then has to raise his head at a ridiculous angle in order to look at you. Equally, you need to be close enough to calmly push his bottom back to the ground if he tries to move off before you have established eye contact. As you will be holding the lead, you will be able to establish the correct position more easily.

If your puppy is still not looking at you once you have moved around a bit, then try a cough or a 'psst' to get his attention. Once he looks at you, immediately praise him and give the next instruction so that he knows you are praising and reacting to the fact that he looked at you.

Whichever way you eventually achieve that first eye contact, work on being able to get it without moving, coughing, or making other suitable noises. This will mean standing still and absolutely silent, perhaps for several minutes. Your puppy must work out that in order to get the next instruction, he has to look at you intently and questioningly.

Once the concept of eye contact has been established, you can move from rewarding him with an instant instruction to holding his gaze for a few moments longer. Beware of going to the other extreme though and making him wait for too long, as he will get bored and eye contact will be lost.

Some dogs just don't get it!

I once helped to train an English Setter bitch. We tried everything to get her to grasp the concept of eye contact and we persisted daily but she never did learn that the secret of being able to RUN ON when out for a walk, was to look up at her owner. Sadly, while she was the sweetest dog, her mental capacity left a lot to be desired!

FIRST WALK

It's important to start as you mean to go on when you take your puppy for his first walk, so that you establish a pattern.

Using a lead for the first time:

1. Decide which side your puppy is going to walk to heel and stick to it. Traditionally this is on the left, because with a gun dog, you will have your gun on your right arm. If you are right-handed, the left is the natural choice and vice versa.

2. Have your lead ready before you call the puppy to you (*for choice of lead see page 16*).

3. Call your puppy to you (remember the no chasing rule).

4. Praise him and give him a pat.

5. Tell him to SIT. To start with, you should still have a gentle hold on him from the cuddle you gave him when he came to you. Then you should gently push his bottom to the ground as you say 'SIT'. Praise him.

6. Quickly slip the lead on. At this stage, he should not be asked to do anything for an extended period. He will soon learn that if he follows a verbal instruction quickly, even if you have had to give physical guidance, he will be rewarded by doing something different.

7. Once the lead is on, say 'HEEL' calmly and quietly and walk off slowly.

HEEL is with your puppy's front legs beside your legs and the lead slack (*see below*). Remember, this is the first time your puppy has been restrained in this way and his natural instinct will be to fight it. He will either drag behind, race ahead, corkscrew around, bite at the lead or a combination!

Initially, just keep him on the lead for a couple of minutes but continue walking slowly as you use both your voice and hands to

try to establish the correct position. Over the course of the next few days and weeks he will gradually become more accepting. Be patient but firm and always start each walk with a brief period on the lead and gradually introduce the concept of eye contact.

After your brief period of lead training, again say 'SIT' and push his bottom down. Remove the lead.

Keeping a gentle hold on him, try to get his attention so that he looks at you (eye contact again). When he does, say 'RUN ON'. He is now free to play.

RUN ON will always be his cue that he is free to go, run free and amuse himself.

Let him have his 10 or so minutes of fun. Keep your walking speed to a stroll, as you do not want your puppy exhausted trying to keep up with you nor do you want to deny him the opportunity to stop and sniff. But, when he does stop and sniff or dash off briefly because something has attracted his attention, do not stop. Keep moving. This is his first lesson in the importance of keeping an eye on you in case he loses you. He will catch you up and when he does, praise him lavishly, encouraging him to come right up to you for praise and cuddles before he goes off again.

LETTING YOUR PUPPY OFF THE LEAD

So many people say, 'But my puppy might run off and I will lose him'. The answer is 'Where will he run to?' He is a baby with no experience of the big wide world and you are the only security he has. Why would he want to lose you? So do not fall into the 'I will keep him on the lead, just in case' trap.

Now is the time, while he is dependent, to get him used to being off the lead so that when he grows older and bolder the rules of the walk will be so well established that his willingness to come back won't be an issue.

A dog that is always on the lead is usually the one who, aged six months and the owner finally decides he is old enough to be let off, takes off and does not come back. Would you like being back on the lead again if you were that dog?

AT THE END OF THE WALK

At the end of the walk, call your puppy back to you, give lots of praise and then follow the same routine as you did at the start of the walk for getting him to sit to put the lead back on. Have just another two or three minutes on the lead on the way back home. This establishes that you are in charge; it provides another opportunity to work on the heel position; it reinforces that walks both start and finish under your control. This is particularly important if you live somewhere where it might not be necessary to put your dog on a lead at all.

WHAT YOUR PUPPY LEARNS FROM A WALK

To walk to HEEL.

To SIT before running on.

To wait before being told to RUN ON.

To look at you – eye contact.

To be aware of where you are.

To come when called.

To socialise with other dogs.

To trust you – he needs you more in unfamiliar territory.

If dogs are allowed to wander out of your garden with you when you are going on a walk, it gives then a strong message that it is fine to wander at will. Soon they will not be waiting for you to come with them!

Dogs that always leave and return to your grounds on a lead are getting a strong message that this only happens under your control. Do not wait until you are out of the garden to put them on a lead. Do it at the back door or somewhere well within the boundary.

MEETING OTHER DOGS ON A WALK

When your puppy first starts going on walks, he is unlikely to stray far from you and may be apprehensive when meeting other dogs. This is good. A measured approach to socialisation will stand him in good stead. Rushing up to a strange dog with no thought could land him in trouble.

Do let him approach other dogs and learn how to socialise. Most dogs are friendly and all will be well. The behaviour of the other dog's owner is your best indicator to the reception your puppy is likely to receive. If all is clearly not well, call your puppy back and beat a hasty retreat. As long as the other dog's owner is relaxed and does not rush to call their dog or put it on the lead, you can assume it is friendly. Do not interfere or put your puppy on a lead, this will only serve to make him feel disadvantaged and threatened should the other dog come up to him.

When you have had enough of standing around, watching your puppy play with his new friend, walk away. Do not start calling him and trying to get him to come to you while you stand still. If he is having fun, he won't take any notice but he will be aware that while you continue to wait for him, he can carry on playing. By walking away and saying nothing until you are at least 25 metres away (and further still if necessary), your puppy should look up, alerted by the silence, see you disappearing and race after you.

If he continues playing, your voice getting further away from him should alert him to look up. You can then call him once more. Do squat down with your arms wide and welcoming and be encouraging while he comes all the way back, then reward him with lavish praise.

COMING ALL THE WAY BACK

He must come all the way back to you in such a situation. Flying past is not acceptable nor is the briefest of 'check-ins'. He must come right up to you, stop and relax while he gets praised. Then, and only then, can you send him on his way once more with a cheery 'Good boy, on you go'.

This is the strategy to maintain as your puppy gets older and bolder and acquires more friends. If you get it right from the beginning, he will have learnt that other dogs are fun but he must keep an eye on you for fear of losing you. If your dog or puppy continues to be difficult about coming back, you should increase the distance you walk away before calling him. Once you have a whistle (*see Whistle Training, pages 89-91*), you will be able to whistle him back from longer distances away.

A rover's return...

A spaniel, aged six months, was brought to me for help. She raced off on walks and didn't come back when called and was beginning to go off for longer and longer periods.

We let her go at the start of our walk, following all the eye contact rules which she grasped in a flash. She raced off at speed and we immediately turned and retraced our steps, out of sight round the corner of a hedge. We said and did nothing more. Two minutes passed and she reappeared. We let her go again and the same thing happened, so we stayed put but she returned in less time.

This continued for a good 20 minutes during which we returned to our place behind the hedge corner as soon as she rushed off. As she began to come back faster and to go away from us more slowly, we were able to move on from our hiding place. In an hour, we had only got 300 metres from our starting point. We had said nothing but this bright, sparky little spaniel had 'got it'.

Apart from one refresher session, that is all it took to transform walks from being stressful and worrying to periods of fun and activity for both owner and dog. It is not always that easy but it is fun just occasionally to resemble a miracle worker!

Do reinforce that 'coming back' is the right thing to do by always being pleased when he reaches you, even if you have had to walk 500 metres and then had to hide! Remember the stop, relax, praise rule before he is allowed to continue running free once again.

CALLING A DEFIANT PUPPY BACK

This is how to get your puppy back to you when he starts pushing the boundaries. It is an approach that can be used in the house, in the garden, or on a walk.

Start by calling the puppy's name in a commanding, but not cross, voice. Always assume he is going to come when you first call him and if you sound assertive and confident there is every chance he will. If he does not come, start using the following 'good cop, bad cop' routine:

1. The 'bad cop' uses a cross, growly type of voice all the time that the puppy is either going away from you or defiantly standing still. The 'bad cop' says things like 'COME HERE AT ONCE', 'DO AS YOU ARE TOLD', 'Here, NOW!' *At no point do you move towards the puppy. You must stand your ground, or move away from him.*

2. The 'good cop' uses an encouraging, praising voice if the puppy so much as takes one step towards you. It is used as long as he continues to move towards you. The 'good cop' says things like 'Good boy, here now', 'Clever boy', etc. The second the puppy stops again or turns away, the 'bad cop' takes over again.

If you have the stamina, keep this up for as long as it takes.

Success at one attempt

My very first puppy who was generally the most amenable and easy puppy in every way, suddenly decided at the age of 12 weeks, in the middle of a cricket pitch, that she was not going to come back. Ten long minutes ensued while I endeavoured to perfect the 'good cop/ bad cop' routine to hoots of laughter from my children then aged six and nine years. Finally, I won and not only was that battle over but the war as well. She never again tried her luck and from then on always came when she was called.

DEMANDING TO COME IN FROM OUTSIDE

Once you have a puppy that can be relied upon to come when he's called in any situation, beware of suddenly finding yourself with a puppy or dog who stands outside the back door barking, whining, or scratching incessantly until you let him in.

How do you teach a dog to let you know he wants to come in? Scratching at the door should be discouraged, as should whining. One bark from outside followed by silence is perfectly acceptable to let you know your puppy is ready to come in, but do not go straight to the door. Leave it a minute or two, or longer if you are in the middle of something, and as long as there is still silence, then he may come in.

Silence is the rule. With a dog making an incessant noise, demanding to come in, the answer is simple: completely ignore him, until he has stopped, before going to the door. Be careful that the silence is not just a pause between barks but a silence that acknowledges that the noise has not worked.

Apart from one bark being acceptable in a well-trained dog, you don't teach him to bark to come in for all the reasons outlined as it can lead to unacceptable and demanding behaviour. Be a good owner and don't forget he is outside in the first place!

Silence is golden...

I once listened to barking, scratching and whining for half an hour before suddenly, there was silence. I left the dog for a further three minutes and then went to the door. As I opened it, I just said, 'Good boy, no noise'. His owners had been responding to the noisy demands for two months but he never again demanded to come in while he was with me!

IMPORTANCE OF SOCIALISING

You must make a point of socialising your puppy with other dogs as soon as possible for the following reasons:

1. He will gain better awareness of how to approach any strange dogs he meets on walks.

2. The best lesson for an over-confident, boisterous puppy who jumps all over an older dog is a warning growl and a baring of teeth from the other dog. Do find a friend who has a dog or bitch that can be trusted to do this without causing harm. An older bitch that has had litters of her own is ideal for this job.

3. Playing is fun but puppies need to learn that rough behaviour can cause pain. They learn to give and take. They also learn to defer to an older dog (e.g. over a stick for which they are competing).

4. It gives them confidence.

5. It is stimulating.

6. It gives them exercise with the freedom to decide when they want to play and when they need to stop and rest.

7. Like us, they need friends and just like us, you will find they like some dogs more than others. Generally, puppies and dogs play the best games with similar types of dog who seem to have an innate awareness of the rules of their game.I have seen this in gun dogs, terriers and guard dogs.

TEACHING YOUR PUPPY TO LIE DOWN

There are times when your puppy should go away and settle down:

- After a session of fun and games
- After a walk
- During the evening
- When you are eating meals
- If he is interrupting children's games

LIE DOWN can be used in two ways:

● **LIE DOWN exactly where the puppy is** when the command is given. With a puppy under six months old it should be easy to push him down gently as you give the command 'LIE DOWN'. The trick is then to keep repeating the process calmly but with authority until he realises he really is going to have to lie down: initially for 10 minutes.

Be realistic in your expectations. Start giving your puppy the command LIE DOWN when you can realistically expect him to stay where you have told him to lie down. Trying to teach an eight-week-old puppy to lie down at all is expecting too much but when he is tired during the evening and ready to sleep is the time to use the command almost as he is settling himself down.

By 12 weeks, it is reasonable for him to start learning to lie down on command during the day; at meal times, for instance. It would be equally ridiculous trying to teach a six-month-old puppy to lie down first thing in the morning when he is full of energy and thrilled to see you. Be realistic, be patient, persistent, and always be consistent.

● **GO AND LIE DOWN when you do not mind where**, as long as it is away from you, e.g. away from the table when people are eating.

6. NEXT STEPS IN TRAINING

FROM ABOUT SIX MONTHS ONWARDS

With all training, it's important not to try to progress too fast. Keep your goals reasonable for the age, maturity and intellect of your puppy. Every puppy is different and will progress at differing rates but the one constant is that they all need to have fully understood and consolidated each instruction before you move on to the next goal.

If your puppy appears confused, suddenly starts getting defiant, loses confidence or interest in his training, it may well be because he does not understand what is required. Take a step back to something he does well. Reinforce it to regain his confidence both in himself and in you. Then, and only then, return to the problem item.

Once you decide on a course of action or give an instruction, you must see it through.

The key remains: **PATIENCE, PERSISTENCE AND CONSISTENCY**

Remember, in all training:
- **KEEP IT SHORT**
- **KEEP IT FUN**
- **MAKE IT VARIED**
- **KEEP IT SIMPLE**
- **MAKE IT CLEAR**
- **MOST OF ALL – REMEMBER TO PRAISE**

WHAT TO EXPECT AND WHEN

The first thing to take into account is what breed of dog you have chosen. **Labradors** mature quickly and will therefore generally be ahead of their **Golden Retriever** friends of the same age. **Flat-coated Retrievers** are the slowest to mature and you can expect the same achievements from a year-old Flat-coat as from an average six-month-old Labrador.

Working Springer and **Cocker Spaniels** do everything fast and that will include racing away from you in every sense unless you get on top of them from a discipline perspective right from the start.

Small dogs mature quickly but you will discover early on that terriers are unlikely to give you the same level of obedience that you can demand from members of the gun dog group of breeds.

There is a huge variation between what one may reasonably expect from a puppy at a particular age, before even starting to consider him as an individual.

AT SIX MONTHS

As a general rule, regardless of breed, and assuming training started early, by six months old your puppy should be able to:

1. Respond to a whistle.
2. Give you eye contact when required.
3. Walk properly to heel on the lead.
4. Respond immediately to the command SIT.
5. Respond immediately to the command LIE DOWN.
6. Respond to the recall whistle (*see pages 89-91*).
7. Be calm and responsive to instruction while being brushed.
8. WAIT on a walk while the lead is taken off until you release him after eye contact with RUN ON.

AT NINE MONTHS

By nine months, it is reasonable to expect a lot more from your puppy. He should be able to:

 1. SIT AND WAIT almost indefinitely and in any situation.

 2. Walk to heel off the lead, properly.

 3. SIT to a whistle command as well as a verbal command.

There will always be exceptions to every rule and the most important part of training a puppy is that you remain:

PATIENT, PERSISTENT AND CONSISTENT

This will allow you to make progress at a speed that suits both you and your puppy.

COPING WITH PROBLEMS

The main thing is not to panic. Most problems can easily be resolved if you take a calm and measured approach. Don't be afraid to ask for help if you need it.

A lot of problems that occur with puppies are caused by mismanagement by their owners. There are also pushy and difficult dogs that cause their owners unnecessary grief. It is often the case that an owner will blame himself for the constant battle with a dog who is always on the lookout for a chink in his armour. A professional trainer will quickly see where the problem lies and be able to offer reassurance.

RULES TO REMEMBER

Formal training should just be an extension of everything you have been doing so far. A lot of work can be done while you are taking the puppy for his daily walks. But always keep these rules in mind:

1. Training should be fun for both you and the puppy.

2. *Patience, persistence and consistency.*

3. Once a command is given, it must be followed through. This may mean endless repetition and it must be achieved in the exact spot where you first made the command.

4. Let a puppy or dog get away with something once and he will try the same thing again and again until you make it clear that your word is law.

5. Always be aware of appropriate use of your voice.

6. You are seeking the cooperation of your puppy, not trying to dominate him.

7. Obedience should be given to you freely by your puppy, not bullied out of him – but there will be arguments along the way!

8. Your puppy should want to please you because he loves and respects you, not because he is frightened of you.

9. Successful training relies on having the full attention of your puppy in order to concentrate on the task in hand.

10. Training should always take place once your puppy has had his exercise for the day. Either following straight on from a walk or later in the day.

11. Do not expect a puppy who has been shut inside all day with no play or walk time to come out and concentrate.

12. Keep training sessions brief. Between five and 15 minutes maximum.

13. You do not have to have a formal training session every day. Every other day, or less, is fine. If you are following the rules for walks, your puppy is, in effect, having a training session each time he goes out.

14. Never try to train a puppy when you are not in the mood and are only doing so because you feel you should. It is a recipe for disaster.

15. Set yourself a realistic target for the day and stick to it.

16. Always end on a high note. Never be tempted to try just one more thing. It usually ends in tears!

17. Always let your puppy have a free play at the end of a session: school is over, now it is break time!

USE OF YOUR VOICE

I am constantly being told that using an appropriate tone of voice and being able to change the expression and mood so that it always suits the current situation are the most difficult parts of training a dog. Take time to think about the tone of voice you should use, think about your puppy's reaction to your voice, and be prepared to change the tone often and quickly. Here are a few tips:

● Never sound pleading when giving your puppy an instruction (e.g. recall).

● Sound authoritative but enthusiastic. If you sound authoritative but cross when calling your puppy to you, he is unlikely to want to come.

● Use a warm voice to praise but keep it calm. Using a high-pitched, excited voice to praise your puppy, who has just sat beautifully to the whistle, will have him jumping around again. On the other hand, a nervous puppy with no confidence needs an enthusiastic, excited voice when you praise him.

● Use a quiet, calm voice to say 'HEEL'. Using a loud enthusiastic voice will have him charging off with you in tow. Being calm and quiet and walking slowly will give a better chance of your puppy keeping to the correct position beside you.

● Use a growly, cross voice when your puppy is not doing as you ask (*i.e. 'good cop, bad cop' routine as described on page 71*) when you are recalling him.

● Use an encouraging voice when you are trying to get your puppy to do something he is clearly not sure about. Be aware of your puppy's mood. Is he refusing to sit and wait because he does not understand what you want? Then use a calm, matter-of-fact voice. Is it because he does not have the confidence to be left

although he thinks it might be what you want? Use an encouraging but calm voice. Does he know perfectly well what you want but is being downright defiant? Use an authoritative, no-nonsense voice.

● Use a cheery voice when you are trying to get your puppy to relax in a situation he clearly finds difficult, e.g. if he is nervous of cars and traffic is going past. A cheery 'Good boy, come on', as you walk purposefully on will tell him there is nothing to worry about. It is usually a mistake to use a soothing, reassuring voice accompanied by stopping and turning or leading him away from the cars in these situations. Your concerned attitude, even if you don't tell him not to worry, will be enough to convince him there is something to be anxious about. If your voice and your physical presence are relaxed and confident, your puppy will be reassured.

ADVANCED HEEL WORK

The second stage of training to heel leads on from establishing a routine for each walk. Heel work started when you first took your puppy for a walk (*see page 65*). Over the following weeks each walk will have provided ample opportunity to perfect the heel position.

Your puppy should be ready to walk to heel off the lead from about nine months old. It is important that you do not try to walk your puppy to heel off the lead until he is walking perfectly to heel all the time on the lead.

If you are tempted to try to get your puppy to walk to heel off the lead while he is still unsure of exactly where 'heel' is when on the lead, 'heel' will very quickly become somewhere in the general vicinity of your legs. You are then unlikely ever to establish the correct position.

Don't be in a hurry. Establish the perfect position for heel and insist on it as soon as the lead goes on. Don't accept pulling at the beginning because he is excited.

Walking properly to heel

Your puppy is walking properly to heel **_when_**:

- His front legs are beside your legs.

- He is close to your legs (remember, your aim is to get dirty trousers!)

- He is walking with the lead slack at all times. Beware of holding him in the correct position with a tight hold on the lead.

- He maintains the correct position, regardless of your speed and direction.

  Beware of matching your speed to your puppy's – you will only fool yourself that you have the whole 'heel' thing perfected.

  Also beware of veering off to either left or right because your puppy has a preference for a desired route and you are inadvertently following him.

If the lead is truly slack (both behind the puppy's neck and between you and the puppy) at all times and you are never having to correct the heel position, then it is time to move to walking to heel off the lead (*see pages 66-67*).

Ironing out problems: walking to heel

If you have not yet achieved the above, the following approaches are helpful for acquiring the correct position.

1. Walk very slowly. This forces your puppy to concentrate.

2. Do not be afraid to pull the puppy back, saying 'HEEL' firmly while you do it. It is the action of the slip lead going from tight to loose that tells the puppy that he is in the correct position.

3. A little flick on the nose with the end of the lead is a good means of gaining attention. It does not hurt but the puppy will not like it and will automatically look up to see what you want. Follow it up with a firm command of 'HEEL'.

4. Vary your speed. Stop and start. This will teach your puppy that he must concentrate on you at all times. Initially, when you stop, exert gentle pressure on the lead so that your puppy stops beside you and not two or three steps in front.

5. Walk in circles both ways. This is a good way to teach your puppy to stay close to your legs as initially you will have to keep pulling him back towards you when he is on the outside leg.

6. Walk in figure-of-eight patterns watching the puppy's position all the time.

7. Weave along in a continuous 'S' shape, varying the sharpness of the turns.

HEEL PRACTICE

- It is essential to do the following exercises slowly.
- Start with circles and progress to figure-of-eight and then S-weaves.
- Do not attempt this off the lead until your puppy walks perfectly in a straight line off the lead and at varying speeds.

CIRCLES

With your puppy on your left, walking to the right in a circle (i.e. clockwise) will be harder as your puppy will be on your outside. As you walk, keep pulling him gently back in beside you.

When going to the left (i.e. anti-clockwise) your puppy will be on your inside, so it will be easier to guide him by nudging him with your leg.

FIGURE-OF-EIGHT

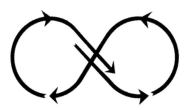

Walking in a figure-of-eight makes your puppy concentrate more as the direction keeps changing.

S-WEAVES

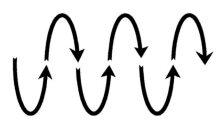

You can vary the speed, size and sharpness of bend while doing S-weaves.

Once you have mastered this...

Now that your puppy is walking perfectly to heel on the lead, the progression to walking off the lead should be very straightforward.

OFF THE LEAD AND WALKING TO HEEL:

1. With the puppy at heel on the lead, slacken the lead round his neck until it is hanging in a large loop which will be very easy to slip off.

2. As you are walking and without altering your natural speed, slip the lead off, saying calmly and quietly, 'HEEL' once. (NB: just dropping the lead onto the puppy's neck achieves nothing.) Make sure you have the lead looped in your hand ready to be slipped back over the puppy's head when required.

3. Your puppy should continue with you in the correct position. If he maintains the correct position, walk ten steps and then slip the lead back on. In this case, go to Step 9.

4. If your puppy rushes forward or hangs back as you slip off the lead, put it straight back on. Do not start saying HEEL and trying to get the puppy to come back into the correct position without the aid of the lead.

5. Walk on a short way until you have re-established the correct position with the lead on and it's slack once again and ready to slip off easily.

6. Say 'HEEL' and try slipping the lead off while you keep walking.

7. If your puppy stays in the correct position, walk ten steps and slip the lead back on as you are walking.

A STEP-BY-STEP PROGRAMME

8. If your puppy is still falling into the wrong position as soon as you slip the lead off, he is not ready to walk off the lead. Go back to *Ironing out Problems* on page 83 and don't take the lead off again for a further two weeks.

9. For those who have managed ten perfect steps with the lead off, on each walk you can gradually increase the time your puppy is at heel off the lead but only do it for as long as he walks in the perfect position.

10. At this stage, you must always start with the lead on and continue to slip it off while you walk.

11. If at any stage your puppy begins to deviate from the perfect position, slip the lead back on and re-establish the correct position. Do not start by trying to get a puppy back into the correct position off the lead. He will become confused and may try to run off and you will get cross and impatient.

    REMEMBER: PATIENCE, PERSISTENCE AND CONSISTENCY

12. Progress slowly and consistently following the rules and it will then be easy.

13. Once he has got the idea and can cope with 20 or 30 metres off the lead at the correct position, a sharp 'Psst' should be enough to bring him back into line should he deviate slightly.

Varying the routine

At this stage you can start varying your routine for the start and finish of walks:

- Tell your puppy to sit while you take the lead off and then say 'HEEL' calmly and quietly and get him to walk to heel, off the lead.

- Instead of slipping the lead back on and having a short time on the lead again before you allow him to 'RUN ON', beep the whistle for him to sit while he is at heel off the lead (*see facing page*). You can then either tell him to 'HEEL' once more or allow him to 'RUN ON'.
  Don't forget eye contact before telling him to 'RUN ON'.

- At the end of the walk, you can start saying, 'Come to heel now' while still walking and see if he can cope with coming and falling into heel beside you without going through the process of getting him to sit first.

- Alternatively, get him to you as you usually do, beep the whistle for him to sit, then say 'HEEL' as you walk off.

If at any stage your puppy starts having trouble maintaining the correct heel position, slip the lead back on and go back a stage in the learning process.

If you get HEEL perfect, you will have control of your dog in any situation.

TRAINING TO THE WHISTLE

Clearly, teaching your puppy to sit to the whistle will require repetitive and consistent use; however, for the purpose of recall, your puppy must view the whistle as an absolute, one-hundred-percent command to come back, not an 'If and when I feel like it' option, so it should always be used sparingly.

I cannot stress strongly enough that silence is your most powerful tool when training your puppy to focus on you, stay with you and come back to you on walks. Follow the whistle instructions with care and always think before you blow.

We use a whistle because:

- It saves shouting.
- The sound carries further than your voice ever could.
- It is more commanding than your voice.
- Dogs are more naturally tuned to the sound pitch of a whistle and will instantly be aware of you, even when there are other noises.
- A whistle on a lanyard around your neck will give you confidence.

Choice of whistle

Whistles may be purchased from any good gun shop or country sports shop. They will usually have a selection in differing pitches (sound frequencies). The most commonly-used ones come in a variety of fun colours, as well as the more traditional black plastic, as manufactured by Acme. They are numbered from 210 to 212, according to pitch. Try them out and pick the one that sounds good to you.

When to start

Start using a whistle as soon as your puppy sits instantly to the command 'SIT' before the lead goes on at the beginning and end of each walk.

When you tell your puppy to 'SIT', follow it immediately by a short, sharp beep on the whistle, always remembering to praise him instantly when he does sit. Gradually, he will realise the whistle beep is a command to sit, the same as the verbal command.

Now you can just use the whistle and omit the verbal command every time you need him to sit. However, do not use the whistle in the house. Once your puppy has understood the meaning of the single beep, you can use the verbal command in the house and the whistle on a walk. Once training advances, there will be plenty of opportunities to reinforce that one short sharp beep means 'SIT'.

Whistle command to return

The most commonly-used signal for calling dogs back is three short, sharp beeps on the whistle. Use just one breath and blow with intent. This is an order for your puppy to 'Come here. NOW'. This is not a polite request or an optional command to be obeyed if your puppy feels like it. Believe me, dogs can tell instantly by the way the whistle is blown whether you mean business or not.

When to use the recall whistle

The recall whistle should be used when your puppy is more than 40 to 50 metres away from you. If your puppy is less than 30 metres away, calling him is the appropriate method of getting him to come back to you. You should have very little need to recall a puppy with a whistle before the age of five months.

As your puppy gains confidence, he will explore further away from you. He will be your guide as to when you need to start using the recall whistle. Five to six months of age is a very general guide, but all puppies vary. As with the whistle command to SIT, start by calling your puppy and using the whistle alternately while he learns what it means.

Make sure your body language is encouraging him to come back as well: crouch down, arms wide with shoulders back. Do not have your arms out in front of you looking as though you are going to grab him.

Possible whistle-training problems

There are a number of problems you may encounter when training to the whistle that may be caused by using it incorrectly. Pay careful attention to the following:

• **Over-use.** Puppies and dogs who are endlessly recalled for no reason other than to reassure their owners that it still works will soon develop selective deafness leading to total disobedience. The whistle always means 'Come back. NOW', so before you use it, think whether you really need your puppy to come back at that moment. Once you blow the whistle, the puppy has to come back to you; not nearly to you or quickly checking in and then shooting on. The return must be right up to you, where he must stop, relax and be praised before he is once more free to go off and enjoy himself.

• **Ignoring the whistle.** This is bound to occur at times either because your puppy is testing whether he really has to obey or because there is something more interesting to distract his attention.

STRATEGIES FOR GETTING YOUR PUPPY BACK

The following strategies apply for any situation where your puppy chooses to ignore the recall whistle. They all serve to teach him that he must keep an eye on you no matter where he is or what he is doing, otherwise he may lose you. Of course you know where he is and you are not going to lose him, but he doesn't know that!

1. Only give the recall signal twice before taking remedial action. Continuous blowing when the puppy is ignoring you will teach your puppy that he can ignore the whistle if he feels like it.

2. Do not call him.

3. Remain silent. Continuous use of the whistle and your voice only serves to reassure your puppy that he can continue with what he is doing in the knowledge that he knows exactly where you are.

4. Retrace your steps and keep going until you are out of sight – one more use of the three-beep recall signal should then serve to help a now hopelessly panicking puppy to see that the whistle has just given him a clue as to where to find you; once he does find you and comes right back to you, be profuse in your praise.

Or continue the way you were going but at an increased speed so that you are not where your puppy thought you might be since he last looked. Once you have gone 75-100 metres, you can use the whistle. Wait until he is looking for you and you can see him, before whistling him to you once again.

Or hide. Trees, bushes and hedges are wonderful allies in the dog-training game. The puppy will look up to check why everything has gone silent and realise he can't see you. Let him panic for a short while and once he is clearly looking for you, depending on distance, either call or whistle him. This will give him a clue to where you are. Again, the whistle will be experienced as a positive contribution to your puppy's enjoyment and not a hindrance or restriction.

Situations in which your puppy might not come back

There are some situations in which your puppy will not return to you immediately, mainly due to distraction:

• **He has found a friend to play with.** If you stand nearby calling endlessly, he will continue playing. In this case use one of the strategies on the facing page. You can also enlist the help of the owner of the other dog by asking them to carry on their way while ignoring your puppy. Should your puppy remain with the other dog and its owner, after you've used your one permitted recall signal, a fierce 'GO AWAY!' from the other owner should help send your puppy back to you.

• **He has spotted something and shoots off after it.** In this case you need him to learn very quickly into the chase that he risks losing you and must start paying attention once more. You do this by remaining silent and following one of the strategies already outlined (*facing page*) for getting your puppy back to you. But do not use the whistle. Let him realise all is quiet and he will then start looking for you. Leave him to get on with it on his own until he finds you. Unless you are intending to train your puppy as a gun dog, chasing the odd rabbit is not a problem but great fun. The problems start when your puppy (who is likely to be six months or over at this stage) chases one rabbit and then moves on to the next, and the next, possibly getting further away from you. By adopting a strategy of complete silence and no whistle, he will learn that after the fun of the initial chase, he must come looking for you or he risks losing you.

• **He is getting older and bolder** and beginning to think he can get away with being further from you for longer periods of time. In this case, use the same approach as when chasing something (*see above*).

TEACHING YOUR PUPPY TO SIT AND WAIT

The command words to WAIT or STAY are both commonly used but I prefer the clear consonant at the end of 'WAIT'. It is more distinct and is firmer and more precise in sound than 'STAY'.

When you come to teaching your puppy to sit and wait, the chances are that you have already started to make progress by:

- Getting your puppy to sit and wait before the lead is put on in preparation for a walk.

- Getting him to sit and wait when the lead is taken off before he is allowed to run free on a walk.

- Getting him to sit and wait and then look at you before he has his food.

First steps in learning how to sit and wait

Five to six months is a good average age to begin teaching your puppy to sit and wait. Remember, all puppies are different and their levels of intelligence, maturity and biddability will determine when they are ready to cope with formal discipline. If your puppy is obviously ready, start earlier.

If your first attempt with your five-month-old puppy is a complete disaster, leave it for two weeks, then try again. Just because a puppy may be slow at one thing, does not mean he will be slow at everything. Beware of getting into a competition with friends who have puppies of the same age.

This exercise should always be done with your puppy on a lead until he has reached the stage of walking to heel without the lead (*see pages 66, 82-87*).

94

1. Tell your puppy to 'SIT'. If he does not respond, gently push his bottom to the ground. Praise him calmly as soon as he is sitting but do not excite him as you do not want him to get up immediately.

2. Wait for him to look at you and immediately say 'HEEL' and walk on.

3. Repeat this exercise a couple of times over a fairly short distance.

4. Tell him to 'SIT' again.

5. Move round so that you are standing directly in front of your puppy and say 'WAIT', firmly but calmly.

6. Gently remove the lead and say 'WAIT' again before moving a couple of steps backwards, away from the puppy.

7. Walk back to him with the lead looped ready to slip over his head as you praise him. Again keep the praise enthusiastic but calming.

8. If all has gone well, walk on a little further with the puppy at heel once more and repeat the exercise, this time taking four steps backwards.

9. Repeat the heel routine and walk a little further.

10. Say 'SIT AND WAIT'. Go round in front of him as before and exactly as you should on each walk and take off the lead.

11. When he looks at you, say 'RUN ON'. This is his playtime. Let him enjoy it for as long as it suits you.

SIT AND WAIT *Step-by-Step*

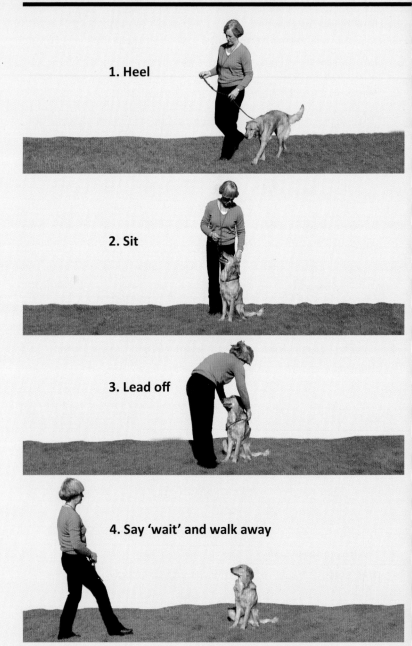

1. Heel

2. Sit

3. Lead off

4. Say 'wait' and walk away

5. Walk away

6. Walk back

7. Lead back on

8. Lavish praise

WHAT TO DO IF YOUR PUPPY DOES NOT WAIT

If you have carefully followed the steps in the exercise, you should have a good prospect of getting your puppy to understand what is required. However, some may take longer to learn to wait. If this happens, do the following:

1. Walk calmly up to him and slip the lead on. If he doesn't let you approach him without fuss do not chase or grab him, walk away or stand still until he eventually comes to you and then slip the lead on.

2. Take your puppy calmly back to the exact spot where you asked him originally to wait.

3. Repeat 'SIT AND WAIT' with the lead off.

4. Again walk two steps backwards.

5. If your puppy looks as if he's going to move, repeat 'WAIT' but be careful not to sound cross, just firm. A cross voice at this point will only worry him and make him more likely to try to come to you for reassurance.

6. If he does move, repeat the last five steps until you succeed, then continue at Step 9 (*page 95*).

7. Your attitude is very important as learning to sit and wait can easily become yet another 'try to catch me' game. If you handle it badly, he will jump around and the whole point of the lesson will be lost. So, remain calm and do not allow yourself to get cross and frustrated.

Some puppies grasp new concepts at once, some find it hard to learn and some don't want to learn. Whatever your puppy's reaction, he needs to understand that this is not a game. He will have to conform in the end. You need to remain calm, cool and authoritative but also reassuring at all times.

SIT and WAIT: points to remember

Each time you take your puppy out for a training session, you can extend the distance you walk away from him, but remember to:

- Keep the distance you walk away restricted to what you feel your puppy is able to cope with.

- Slow, positive advancement is far better than undermining both your own and your puppy's self confidence by trying to go too fast and expecting too much.

- Never, at this stage, leave your puppy sitting and waiting and then call him to you. You want him to accept that waiting is something he does until you come back to him. A puppy who sits and waits and is then called will always be inclined to anticipate the recall and will often 'jump the gun', eventually responding to your body language rather than the actual recall.

- Always walk away looking at your puppy. If you turn your back, you won't see if he moves and a game of 'Grandmother's footsteps' may be under way!

MAKING PROGRESS

Once you can walk approximately 30 metres away from your puppy and back to him without his moving a muscle, you can proceed to the next stage:

1. Try walking a short way past in the other direction before you return and praise him. Say 'WAIT' as you walk past him, just as a reminder.

2. Increase the distances until you can go 25 metres both ways.

3. Now try walking in a circle around your puppy while he sits and waits. Dogs find this very difficult as you keep moving but are always at the same distance from them. Initially, keep the circle small – just 2 metres from your puppy. Gradually increase the circumference of the circle until you are eventually 25 metres away.

4. Shifting around on the spot in order to be able to see you is quite permissible for your puppy but leaving the spot is not.

5. Remember, if your puppy moves you must ensure he is returned to the exact spot where you asked him to wait. The exercise is repeated until he gets it right but you can reduce the distances involved, as it is the concept that a command once given has to be obeyed that matters.

Trust – a saving grace

A trained dog puts his trust in his owner and has also acquired self-control. With a gun dog this can mean not chasing rabbits. You can teach a dog that it should not chase 'fur' but without self-control, the dog is unlikely to ignore rabbits when it is running free at a distance from you.

Self-control and trust can also save a dog from serious injury. Out shooting one day with one of my Golden Retrievers, then aged only two, just such a situation arose. She was out working at a distance from me when she jumped a ditch and then tried to jump the fence beyond it. The fence was in a state of disrepair and made of barbed wire. I was horrified to see that she had become entangled in the wire and was suspended from it. I immediately yelled, 'KEEP STILL. WAIT. I AM COMING' and rushed to her aid. Her natural instinct must have been to struggle to free herself, which would have increased the risk of injury, but she did not move a muscle and I was able to free her without her sustaining so much as a scratch.

A few weeks later, our family was out tobogganing with another family. In the chaos and excitement, the same Golden Retriever was hit hard by a toboggan. I said nothing but she just stood still and waited for me to come to her. I checked her over and reassured her that no damage had been done and we joined the fun once more.

Were the two incidents connected? I will never know but her behaviour throughout her life in many different situations makes me think they were.

By George – he's got it!

There will be a moment, while you are teaching your puppy to sit and wait, that his posture relaxes and you realise that he has 'got it' and no matter how far you go away from him, he will remain firm.

When you reach this point and have successfully completed all the exercises, use this newly acquired skill in real-life situations. Do not keep on and on doing more exercises for the sake of it. Your puppy will get bored and so will you! Occasionally, when out on a walk, give your puppy a refresher exercise in sitting and waiting but keep it brief, do not labour the point and keep it fun with lots of praise at the end.

Once you are confident that your puppy will consistently obey your command to WAIT, you can use it in a variety of situations:

- 'WAIT' before telling your dog to get into the car.
- 'WAIT' when you open the boot to put things in with the dog but do not want him to come out.
- 'WAIT' when he is dirty or wet after a walk. He can wait in the room you specify without you having to shut him in.
- 'WAIT' out in the garden even though the door is open so that he is not in your way.
- 'WAIT' in the house or the car while you load and unload. It saves opening and shutting doors the whole time.
- 'WAIT' until you tell him to get out of the car.
- 'SIT AND WAIT' while you let cars or people in and out of open gates.
- 'WAIT' on his bed if you need him to.

The possibilities are endless and just learning to WAIT could one day save his life. While he is sitting and waiting, it will be someone else's dog who rushes through the open gate onto a busy road in front of a car.

The ultimate wait

I was out training with my mother and our entire Golden Retriever family, including my then 11-year-old bitch, Killie. As usual, all but the dog that was being handled were told to sit and wait. The retrieve did not go as planned and we ended up going over a fence, that would have been beyond Killie's capabilities, and then on into another field. We took the younger dogs with us but Killie was told to sit and wait.

To my shame, by the time the retrieve was over, I had forgotten about poor Killie and we walked home by a different route. After 20 minutes, her absence was noticed with a sense of panic. Where was she? Had she set off for home? Had she gone to look for us elsewhere? No... On returning to where she had been told to wait, there she still sat in exactly the same spot. It takes tremendous discipline and trust in the owner to wait that length of time. Never has a dog had so much praise from such a guilt-ridden owner!

With the best will in the world it is almost impossible to have a seamless trouble-free time training a puppy. Problems will occur along the way and the more strong-willed your puppy is, the more likely it is that you will struggle with some of the training. The trick is not to ignore a problem or difficulty but to take decisive action immediately before a small issue becomes a major problem. Not coming back is a classic example.

This chapter should set you back on track but if it doesn't, my advice is to seek professional help and not waste valuable time before doing so!

CHEWING

Puppies need to chew, particularly when they are losing their baby teeth and the adult teeth are erupting. Chewing is an important aid to muscle development. But some puppies chew more than others and often it's anything they can get their teeth into such as furniture, shoes, clothes.

When buying a puppy, if you ask the breeder whether the puppy's mother was a chewer or if she knows about the father, you will get a pretty good idea as to how easily (or when) the chewing is likely to stop.

Possible causes

Other reasons your puppy might be chewing items on the forbidden list are:

- **Boredom** A puppy left alone for long periods without any stimulation is likely to amuse himself by chewing the furniture or a shoe left lying in a convenient place. Go to the butcher and buy any large raw meaty bone. Marrow bones are also perfect. They provide hours of fun, muscle development and teeth cleaning. Now when you go out, your puppy has a treat to look forward to.

- **Lack of exercise** Once your puppy reaches the age of five or six months, it's important that he has had an appropriate amount of exercise before being left alone in the house. He will then not have any pent-up energy to let go. In the morning, it's unwise to leave the puppy while you do the school run and then go on to the supermarket and coffee with a friend before finally returning home to take him for a walk. Get up earlier and walk the dog before breakfast. 'I did not have time' is never an excuse for not exercising a dog: make time.

- **Diet** A puppy fed exclusively on dried food does not get the opportunity to chew as the food pellets are swallowed too quickly.

Deterrents against chewing

You will have realised by now that the solution is to give your puppy raw, meaty bones. Even better, you should give serious consideration to changing his diet completely, taking advice from your vet.

Alternatively, obtain a supply of hide bones from your pet shop but beware of the shoe-shaped ones. Puppies have difficulty in differentiating between these and the real thing. Choose the ones with a knot at each end. They come in various sizes to suit all breeds and ages. Dried pigs' ears and other similar delicacies are fine but they are high in calories and you will need to adjust your puppy's food accordingly.

If your puppy persists in chewing skirting boards, the edges of cupboards, etc., try making a foul concoction of mustard, chilli powder, and other very hot-tasting ingredients and smear it on the places he chews.

How to teach your puppy that chewing is not acceptable

It is a generally-held principle that you cannot successfully reprimand a dog or puppy unless you catch him in the act. However, in my experience, it is possible to indicate that chewing is not acceptable when you return to find the puppy has caused damage. In this case, it is essential that the reprimand is done as soon as you spot the damage:

1. When you enter the house, don't greet the puppy or make eye contact until you've seen there has been no damage.

2. If you see new damage, take the puppy by the scruff and pull him to the spot and say in a very cross manner, 'What is this? What have you done?'

3. Put his face right up to the damage and say 'NO' again, firmly and crossly. A smack on the bottom does not go amiss at this point. Clear up any mess in front of him.

4. Then take the puppy and put him outside.

5. After 10 minutes, let him in. The incident is now over and he has to be forgiven, so reassure him and then carry on as normal. Do not be tempted to keep scolding or reminding him of the matter every time the damage catches your eye. It is very important that puppies and dogs have a clear indication when things start and stop and that includes being told off.

6. Should the puppy forget and chew again the next time you are out, he will probably look guilty when you return. He will

certainly look very guilty and ashamed when you deliver the 'What have you done?' line.

7. It may take a few attempts but by following the same procedure, all but the most persistent and defiant puppies will acquire the self-control not to chew. At best you will have a puppy that never chews and at worst, even the most persistent offenders, with increasing maturity, will grow out of it.

DESTRUCTIVE BEHAVIOUR

Most destructive behaviour involves chewing and it occurs when the puppy is alone. However, some, if not given clear guidelines early enough, will happily take shoes and chew them, steal washing from the basket, pull down coats from hooks or which have been left on chairs. Some puppies then chew the stolen items, others just take them off, often into the garden, and dump them.

Learning to LEAVE IT

The cure for both sets of behaviour is the same: it is important to teach the puppy what things he is allowed to have and what is forbidden. Arm yourself with a selection of forbidden items and drop one near to the puppy, saying, 'LEAVE IT' firmly at the same time. Other than ensuring that he does leave them alone, do not make the puppy sit or interfere in what he is doing while you do this. If he does make a grab for the item, be sure to get to it first and snatch it up, saying 'NO' firmly, as you do it. Then drop the item again, repeating the instruction to 'LEAVE IT'.

If your puppy ignores the item, praise him and then drop a second item, repeating the same process, saying 'LEAVE IT' and, if necessary, grabbing the item before he does. This can be repeated until the entire floor is littered with shoes, balls, socks, etc., and the puppy becomes so overwhelmed that he can no longer cope and gives up completely.

He has now learnt the command 'LEAVE IT' in addition to understanding that there are items sometimes left lying around which he cannot have.

Follow the same process for a puppy that pulls things off chairs or tables, only place the items enticingly on the furniture instead.

Once you have taught your puppy to leave things that you do not want him to have, it is important that you remain vigilant for a while in case he is tempted again. In this case, a warning 'DON'T YOU DARE' should serve as a reminder if he so much as looks at a forbidden item, particularly if it is swiftly followed by a firm 'LEAVE IT'.

If your puppy does get hold of a forbidden item, refer back to the chapter *Early Days* (*see pages 26 and 31*) to ensure that all the rules are followed correctly while you get your puppy to give the item back.

STEALING FOOD

My first question to people who ask why their puppy steals food is 'What diet is he on?' So far, all the people I have asked have told me they feed their dog on dried food.

Ask yourself: would you steal the delicious smelling roast chicken from the kitchen if you had nothing to eat other than a few pellets in the bottom of a bowl each day? Just giving your dog raw meaty bones to chew as a supplement to his dry diet might be enough to stop the stealing. Otherwise, providing hide bones might help.

Completely changing the puppy's diet, according to your vet's advice, is most likely to cure the problem but if you feel the additional work that might be involved in a total change of diet is not for you, the following strategies should help:

1. Get yourself an empty tin or other 'noisy' receptacle and fill it with small stones.

2. Leave something enticing on the table or sideboard.

3. Leave the room but make sure you can see your puppy. He will almost certainly be looking to see if the coast is clear before he makes his grab!

4. As the puppy goes to steal the food, shake the tin. The noise should shock him into stopping.

5. You can progressively make the food more available, even going so far as to put it on the floor but do have it on an easily recognisable plate that is normally used for human food.

6. Continue to shake the tin vigorously each time the puppy so much as looks at the food. Continue until he gets the message that any thought of touching it is forbidden.

Alternatively, place the food in enticing and available locations and follow the procedure described on pages 107-108 using the commands 'DON'T YOU DARE', 'LEAVE IT', and 'NO'.

PERSISTENT JUMPING UP

Many owners find that preventing their puppies or dogs from jumping up on people – either themselves, visitors or other walkers – is one of the most difficult problems to solve. Your cute puppy is by now probably a robust six-month-old so decisive action must be taken.

- Firstly, does your voice really sound as if you mean it when you tell your puppy to 'GET DOWN'?

- Are the children still waving their arms in the air as the puppy approaches, giving a clear signal to the puppy to jump up?

- Are you letting the puppy put his feet up on you in other situations, to give him affection perhaps? A puppy, unlike a child, can't be taught that something is fine in one situation but not in another.

- Are some people telling him to get down but not, crucially, everyone?

Smacking

One meaningful whack on the nose with a rolled up newspaper accompanied by a ferocious 'GET DOWN' should do the trick. Remember you are not going to continue whacking him on the nose, nor should you, so make it clear that keeping four feet on the ground is for ever not just the next five minutes until he fancies jumping up on somebody else!

If you have a friend – preferably one the puppy doesn't know very well – who is prepared to use the rolled up newspaper, leave the paper outside the door and ask the friend to be verbally ferocious and use the rolled up paper with intent when she/he arrives!

Your puppy will then think pretty hard about jumping up in future.

People worry that they will hurt their puppy smacking him on the nose in this manner. Believe me the only thing you will hurt are his feelings which is nothing compared to a flattened two-year-old child or an elderly person who ends up with a broken hip because you were too feeble to stop your dog from jumping up.

PROBLEMS WITH HOUSE TRAINING

If your puppy still doesn't understand he must go outside to relieve himself, it is probably because you are inadvertently giving him mixed messages.

While it is sensible to put newspaper down for the first couple of weeks for him to use overnight, he has to learn to hang on until you come down to let him out in the morning. By the time the puppy is 10 weeks old and certainly by the time he is 12 weeks old, you should cease to use newspaper. You may still get the occasional accident but he needs to be made aware that this is no longer acceptable:

• When you first come down in the morning, do not greet your puppy until you have checked for accidents. If you find a pee, take him gently by the scruff of the neck to the wet patch, push his nose down towards it and firmly say 'NO'. Without saying anything further, take him to the door and put him out. Encourage him to perform and praise him when he does. Once he comes inside, the incident is over and you can make a fuss of him as you normally would when you first see him in the morning.

• If you are at home with him, do not leave any newspaper down during the day, even when he first arrives. If, as is usual, your puppy has been trained to use newspaper, its continued availability tells him that it is acceptable to relieve himself in the house.

- If you are going out for more than two hours, it is sensible to leave newspaper on the floor but clear it up as soon as you return. If the newspaper is dry, make a big fuss of your puppy and get him outside quickly. Do remember to praise him once he pees outside. If the newspaper has been used, take the puppy outside and praise him when he pees but make no reference to the pee inside, just quietly clear it away.

If your puppy is persistently peeing on the carpet, follow the same procedure for when you find a pee on the floor in the morning. It is important the misdemeanour is pointed out to your puppy, even if it is after the event. Take him gently by the scruff of the neck to the evidence, push his nose towards it and say 'NO' firmly. Then take him straight outside and unless you are sure the accident was very recent, encourage him to do a pee and be lavish in your praise when he does.

Thoroughly clean the soiled carpet to ensure no smell remains. Puppies always return to the same place if there is any lingering scent. Several commercial products are available to remove the smell of pet soiling.

Remember to praise your puppy every time you see him perform outside, particularly if you are having problems. It is very important that your displeasure at his messing inside is balanced by positive reinforcement when he gets it right.

NOT COMING BACK ON WALKS

It is usually from about six months of age that the problem of not coming back to you when you call on a walk can start. Your puppy has grown into a young dog and no longer feels dependent on you and has acquired the confidence to explore. There are several reasons why a dog ceases to think it's necessary to come back to you when called:

1. He was kept on a lead and never allowed to run free during his early days, i.e. the period when the last thing he wanted to do was to lose sight of you. Now, at six months, he has finally been set free. Would you come back and risk being put on the lead again?

2. Owners are generally meticulous in telling their dogs which way they are going on walks. They tend to call him at every junction and turn to ensure they don't lose him. All the time you are calling and whistling, the dog knows exactly where you are and so can carry on doing as he wants in the sure knowledge that he can find you. Even better are those owners who stop and wait for their dogs to come back into view to let them see which way to go. Why should the dog bother to check in when the owner is so accommodating?

3. Owners who constantly call their dogs while out on a walk rarely make them come right back to them. These dogs are probably ignoring their owners and learning that they don't have to respond when they hear their name.

4. The other scenario is where the dog returns and then runs straight past, never stopping to check in properly. If he discovers he can do this, he will start flying past at an ever-increasing distance until the day when he thinks he does not have to come at all.

5. Similar problems occur with over-use of the whistle.

RE-TRAINING YOUR PUPPY OR DOG TO COME BACK ON WALKS

No matter how the problem started, the cure is the same and relies on teaching the dog that he must pay attention and keep an eye on you so that he does not lose you. He needs to do the worrying, not you! To achieve this:

1. Apart from giving praise when the dog is right beside you, maintain silence on walks.

2. No longer tell your dog which way you are going: just go. This requires holding your nerve, as your dog may take a while to realise you have vanished and he is no longer getting reassuring updates on your position.

Remember all dogs have noses which they can use with remarkable effect. Your dog will eventually return to where he last saw you and then follow the line of your scent trail until he finds you. There may be a bit of racing around and panic until he works out what he has to do but he will get there in the end.

If you can see your dog at this point and it is clear he is actively looking for you, either call or whistle (*see Training to the Whistle on pages 89-93*) to aid him in his search. When he comes to you, he must come all the way to you and stop and relax long enough to be praised before you tell him he can 'RUN ON' again. This rule applies whether or not you have helped him to find you. It is of fundamental importance. Do not make him sit. Keep the objective clear and simple.

Every time your dog comes back to you and receives lavish praise without being made to sit, be put on a lead, or any other infringement of his liberty, he is learning that coming back is desirable and rewarding.

3. You are now going to become even more unpredictable. As soon as your dog is no longer within a zone in which he feels comfortable or if he dashes off in an out-of-control manner, vanish! You can achieve this by either:

- Darting sideways and finding a suitable hiding place.
- Continuing on your planned route but at a greatly increased pace so that you will not be where your dog expects to find you.
- Turning and retracing your steps at speed.
- Making an unscheduled turn which your dog will not be expecting and keep going.

Whichever option you choose, keep silent, hold your nerve and wait. I have waited for up to 12 minutes sometimes and have resorted to clutching my whistle in my hand to stop myself blowing it but I have never lost a dog yet.

When your dog does return to you, remember he must come right back to you, stop, relax and receive lavish praise.

Even if you have waited 15 minutes the first time and nearly had heart failure, do not be tempted to put your dog back on the lead. This will teach him that it was not worth coming back after all.

Similarly, never be cross with a dog that has come back. There is one exception to this rule given at the end of this section. It is for owners of dogs that can be left sitting and waiting almost indefinitely. Unless this applies to you, you can never afford to be cross. If you are, your dog will have absolutely no desire to return as you are, in effect, punishing him for the last thing he did, i.e. coming back!

4. Depending on how bad the problem has become, in the initial stages, you may spend a lot of time hiding, running and waiting. Be patient: this approach has never failed me. Sometimes dogs or puppies can be reformed in just one walk. Generally, the younger they are, the easier it is to resolve it. Once they realise they have to concentrate on you, the time it takes for them to find you gets shorter and shorter. An 18-month-old dog who has had months of doing exactly as he likes will take longer to reform. Even if the final result is not perfect, then patience, persistence and consistency will lead to a huge improvement.

WHEN TO RECOMMENCE CALLING OR WHISTLING

During the period of retraining, the best time to recommence calling or whistling is:

- When you know your dog is looking for you.
- On any occasion when you see your dog racing back towards you from a distance. However, remember to follow through on the 'right back to me' routine and crouch down with your arms wide open in an encouraging and positive manner but be careful not to lean forward looking as though you are going to grab him. Keep your arms out but shoulders back.
- When your dog is at a distance and looks towards you and is not distracted by anything and you are confident that he will come if asked.

All these things reinforce that coming back is both positive and rewarding and that the whistle or your voice are a help and not a hindrance to his enjoyment of walks. Once these stages have been completed, you should be able to call or whistle whenever you really do need your puppy back and he will come willingly to you.

Whistle: words of warning

- Do not overuse the whistle to reassure yourself that it still works.
- Only call or whistle if you are prepared to follow it through.
- Remember that silent walks are the best walks.
- In any situation, call or whistle twice at most and then revert to silence and appropriate evasive action.

WHAT TO EXPECT FROM DIFFERENT BREEDS ON WALKS

Do take account of the breed of your dog. While most breeds can reasonably be expected to be within sight most of the time, some are bred to range further.

For example, Pointers and Setters naturally hunt at distance, so don't expect them to potter around your feet like most Golden Retrievers and Labradors. Spaniels have a huge work ethic and are always on the go but this shouldn't be half a mile away. Lurchers, Greyhounds and Whippets hunt with their eyes and once they see prey, they will be gone. You won't stop them, so don't whistle or call. If you get the training right, they will come back to you once their quarry has gone to ground. Terriers are unlikely to be deterred from the chase but they too will come and find you again, especially if there is silence – it really is golden!

DOGS WHO WON'T COME BACK BUT WHO WILL SIT AND WAIT

This is an alternative strategy particularly suited to dogs that come back but only after the second or third time of asking. If, and only if, you have a dog who can be trusted to sit and wait while you walk a minimum of 75 to 100 metres away, you may then break the rule of never being cross when he does eventually come back.

When your dog takes longer than you would like to come back:

1. Do not offer any praise or encouragement as he comes towards you.

2. When he gets to you, pick him up by the scruff with both hands on either side of his neck, lift his front legs off the ground.

3. Say words to the effect of 'BAD DOG, WHERE HAVE YOU BEEN?'

4. Plonk him back on the ground.

5. Say 'SIT AND WAIT' firmly.

6. Walk 75 to 100 metres away, or further, but you need to be sure that your dog will not leave the spot as it is very important that no side issue arises with you struggling to get him to sit and wait.

7. Whistle or call him to you being hugely positive and encouraging during the entire time it takes for your puppy to reach you.

8. Once he gets to you, be over the top in your praise and then tell him he can once again 'RUN ON' freely.

The message this strategy gives is that you were not cross because he came back; you were cross because he did not come straight back. This works on any reasonably bright and fundamentally well-trained dog. If you are in any doubt that your dog could get confused or not understand the point being made, stick to the strategies described previously.

WHEN YOUR DOG WON'T COME ALL THE WAY BACK

Usually, the case of not coming all the way back to you applies to dogs who have been constantly grabbed at or 'caught' rather than being made to come the whole way up to their owners every time they are called. The chances are this occurs both at home and out on walks when it is time for the lead to go back on.

For help with solving this problem in the home or garden, refer to the chapter *Early Days* (*Learning His Name, page 26; Games, page 29; Coming When Called, page 33*). To solve the problem of not coming right back to you when out on walks, use the following procedure:

1. Vary the point where you get your puppy back to you to put him on the lead.

2. Call your puppy firmly and authoritatively to you but beware of sounding cross.

3. If he starts coming towards you, be encouraging but beware of sounding as if you are pleading.

4. If he then turns away or stops, re-issue the command to come but at this point you can sound both very firm and cross, saying 'COME HERE NOW. DO AS YOU ARE TOLD'.

5. If he comes, revert to being pleased and encouraging.

6. You now need him to come all the way to you. Do not be tempted to make a grab for your puppy once you think he is within reach. This is what he will be hoping for and he will always win this game.

7. Keep your hands down (behind your back if necessary), crouch down with your knees bent and look welcoming.

8. If he comes all the way, praise him and keep a firm but light hold on him. You do not want him darting off while you

sort out the lead but neither do you want him to feel trapped. You should be holding him in a rewarding and affectionate manner.

9. Slip the lead on and off you go.

10. But, if this has not worked and your puppy has not come to you at the second time of asking, turn and walk away slowly. The idea is to cover as little ground as possible so that your puppy does not, in effect, get an additional walk while you use the 'walking away' technique.

11. Say nothing and keep walking in the opposite direction.

12. If he follows, wait for an appropriate moment and turn back towards him, crouch down, look welcoming, keep your hands down (remember – no grabbing) and wait to see if he is going to come. If he does, great! Follow the instruction from Step 5 (*page 119*).

13. If he does not come to you, use the following strategy *but keep silent*. Keep walking slowly away from your puppy until he comes past you from behind. At this point, turn immediately and walk *very slowly* in the opposite direction. *Keep silent, walk slowly*, and just keep turning and walking in the opposite direction each time your puppy passes you for as long as it takes for your puppy to work out that this game is no longer fun.

Your puppy will eventually give in and come to you. The moment of defeat is usually very obvious: the body sags, the tail goes down as he approaches, his whole demeanour will say, 'I give in. You win. I can't take any more.'

This strategy will give your dog the strong message that you are no longer 'playing the game' and that you won't plead, you won't chase and you won't grab.

Now put on the lead following Steps 8 and 9. Even though you may feel like killing your dog at this point, don't: you must praise him even if it is through gritted teeth!

You will not be out of the woods yet, so be prepared for a few more sessions, which are likely to be just as bad before things start to improve; but improve they will and the time you take to win will decrease until you have won not only the battle but the war as well!

Persistence pays!

The worst case I have ever dealt with was with a Labrador. On day one of her residential training with me, it took 45 minutes in torrential rain using every strategy previously described before she finally came right up to me with head bowed and let me slip on the lead. It was never as bad again and she went home six weeks later a reformed and amenable character.

Other points to consider

● It is tempting with a young dog that won't come all the way back, to put the lead on too early in the walk. The dog has come back thinking it is safe from being caught but no, you have slipped the lead on just in case you cannot get hold of him at the end. *Do not do this.* The more you can get your dog to come back and have a cuddle during the walk without being put back on the lead, the more likely you are to get his cooperation at the end of the walk.

● While you sort out this problem, do not fall into the 'I have only got 20 minutes to walk the dog' trap. Nothing will lead to frustration and failure quicker than not allowing enough time to follow the strategy to a satisfactory conclusion.

● Go for a walk when you intend to walk for half an hour but when you have one and a half hours before your next engagement.

IN THE CAR

There are three types of problems with puppies in cars:

1. The puppy who does not like being in the car, who probably drools incessantly and is also sick.
2. The puppy who jumps over from the back of the car onto the back seat or from back seat to front when the car is moving or when he is left for a while when it is parked.
3. The puppy who barks in the car:
   - At things he sees out of the window
   - Because he's over excited in expectation of what is to follow (e.g. a walk)
   - Because he does not like being put in the back of an estate or hatch-back car.

The unhappy or sick puppy

If your puppy is unhappy or sick when travelling in the car:

1. Avoid feeding him just before you go out in the car.
2. If you have had him in a cage in the car, try doing without it. Sometimes it is just the feeling of being enclosed in a cage that makes being in the car an unpleasant experience.
3. If you have been using a cage, make sure it is not too small. It may have been perfect when the puppy was younger but how much has he grown?
4. Can your puppy see out of the window from his position in the car? This is a good reason to have a grill fitted rather than having the dog confined to a cage.

5. Does the puppy have something to lie on which prevents him from sliding around?

6. Are you taking the puppy in the car often? If not, do so, particularly for short journeys and even better, on journeys where there is something positive for him to enjoy at the other end – a walk or playtime with a canine friend.

7. Try giving him something to chew in the car: either a hide bone or a raw meaty bone. This provides a good distraction and sometimes just the fact that it is chewing can stop a puppy being sick.

8. Be positive and upbeat as you put your puppy in the car. Saying 'It's all right, not a long journey. Oh poor boy, etc.,' will only make him feel justified in his belief that the car is unpleasant. On the other hand, a cheery 'Come on, in the car. We are off for a WALK' will have the opposite effect.

9. In extreme cases, you can try feeding your puppy in the car with the tailgate or doors open to start with.

10. Get the children to play games with the puppy in the car or through the open doors when the car is parked at home.

With perseverance, all dogs can be cured. It is just a matter of working out what's causing the problem and over time, turning the puppy's negative thoughts about the car into positive ones.

Barking in the car

If your puppy barks out of excitement or frustration, ignore him but each time the barking starts, stop the car. If he does not stop barking quickly, then turn off the engine as well.

It is a good idea to plan your first journey carefully as you may need to stop frequently. It is important that you resist the temptation to talk to, or to yell at your puppy. He needs to learn that barking does not work. Once he is quiet, start the car again and move off, repeating the strategy as many times as is necessary. Take a book or newspaper with you!

Moving about in the car

The obvious solution is to buy a cage or get a grill fitted to the car. This is also the safest solution. Despite this, I don't use cages for my own Golden Retrievers as they enjoy stretching out in the rear of the car.

When you put your puppy in the car, make sure you tell him to 'WAIT' as you close the door. If your puppy jumps over while the car is in motion, stop the car, open one of the back doors to get to your puppy and push him firmly back, saying 'WAIT THERE' as you do it. Sound as cross and authoritative as you can! The same applies if he appears in the front – always push him back over rather than going to the back and trying to call or entice him back to the correct place.

You may need to stop a few times on the first journey but he should quickly get the message. The more meaningful you sound, the fewer times you will have to stop and repeat the procedure. So far, I have never had to stop more than three times, even with the worst offenders.

If your puppy is fine in the back while the car is in motion but hops over to a more comfortable seat once your back is turned, find somewhere to park where you can see the car but your puppy can't see you once you have left it. Leave him in the car with a firm 'WAIT THERE'. Walk away but keep glancing back as you need to be ready to race back as soon as he jumps over onto his favoured seat. At this point, go and push him back over with a very cross and firm, 'WAIT THERE WHEN YOU ARE TOLD'.

Keep doing this just as an exercise until he stays put for at least five minutes: then go back to the car, open the rear door and praise him lavishly for waiting when he was told and then get him out of the car.

Once you have achieved this parked in a place where you can watch him, it is then time to try it on the supermarket run. Remember to tell him to 'WAIT THERE' as you leave the car. Praise him when you get back if he has not moved but be prepared to say nothing, other than 'YOU WAIT THERE' as you push him back over if he has again hopped into the front.

STATIC ELECTRIC COLLAR – THE LAST RESORT

The static electric collar works by giving the dog an electric shock when the behaviour is inappropriate and, unlike the freedom fence collar (*see page 11*), is controlled by the handler.

There is much talk about banning collars on the grounds of cruelty. My opinion is that they should never ever be used as an alternative to good training methods but used appropriately they can literally be a life-saver.

If a dog habitually chases sheep and all other methods of training have failed, then it is surely better for him to get a short sharp shock than to be shot dead by an outraged farmer. It is absolutely within the farmer's rights to shoot a dog worrying sheep on his land.

Dogs who eat stones and find themselves at the vet having operations to remove them can be similarly trained with appropriate use of an electric collar. There is only a certain amount of times that a dog can undergo the same surgical procedure, so the choice might be a shock or euthanasia.

WHO IS IN CHARGE?

Very few people tend to have just one problem with their puppy or dog and it all goes back to: who is in charge? Dogs are great at spotting any chinks in the armour of their owners. Just being a bit slack in one area of discipline usually leads to dogs pushing the boundaries in others. The dog that barks in the back of the car also pulls on the lead and probably won't wait either.

Do not just tackle one problem in isolation. Think about any other area where discipline is slack and put in a zero tolerance regime. Every area of behaviour impacts on all other areas. It can all easily come apart, it can just as easily be put right.

In addition to obvious areas of discipline and training, such as

- Walking to heel
- Sitting and waiting
- Coming when called and whistled
- Lying down when told

think about other areas where you might have inadvertently elevated your puppy up and out of his position at the bottom of the family hierarchy.

- Is he being allowed to sit on chairs and sofas at his discretion?
- Is he sitting up next to you in front of the car?
- Is he barging past you to get through doors?
- Is he pushing in or out of the house ahead of you?
- Is he diving into his food bowl before it has even hit the ground?
- Are you feeding him tit-bits?
- Is he incessantly trailing around the house after you rather than lying quietly (particularly when he should be tired and settled after a walk).
- Is he jumping in or out of the car before you tell him he can?

The dog who had trained his owner

I was asked to train a nine-month-old chocolate Labrador who, I was told, was simply in need of some basic discipline. This was true where outside training was concerned. What the owner didn't tell me was that he had to get up at 5am every day to let the dog out or he would pee in the house. Even worse, unless the owner got dressed and went outside with the dog, he would refuse to pee outside and do it inside as soon as he got back in. The dog had trained his owner to a high standard as he got his way all the time!

Such a situation can occur quite innocently. At some stage, the dog had needed to go out rather early, so had barked. He had been let out and the owner had gone with him to check if it was a real emergency.

It happened again the next morning and the owner responded, fearing an accident if he did not. At this point, unless the dog was known to have a severely upset stomach, he should have been ignored. This young, it is unlikely he would have made a mess or peed out of defiance. If he had been ignored and he had made a mess of any description other than what was clearly unavoidable, the dog should have been taken to the mess by the scruff of the neck and clearly told his behaviour was unacceptable. He should then have been shoved out of the back door and ignored for half an hour. When let back in, the incident should be considered as over. However, this wasn't the case and things went from bad to worse.

How did I cure it? I started by getting up an hour later than 5, with the plan that the time would gradually be extended as the training progressed until I could safely leave it until 8am or later if I wanted.

more...

The dog did bark on the first morning. I ignored it and he stopped but he had peed by the time I came down. I took him by the scruff of the neck, rubbed his nose in it and generally made it clear by what I said and how I said it that his behaviour was unacceptable. Without saying anything more, I shut him in my dog run outside. (Any shed, enclosure, or other isolated place will do just as well.) I left him for half an hour leaving the back door open so he could hear me noisily feeding the other dogs their breakfast.

As a protest, the dog took to lying on my favourite armchair, but after three mornings of admonishment and exclusion time, he stopped lying in my chair. At 7.30am the next day, there was no pee and he gave me a rapturous welcome, clearly indicating, 'Look, I have been a good boy!' We had one relapse before he went home and I followed exactly the same procedure. He eventually returned to his owner completely cured.

If you have followed all the advice in this guide and been both persistent and patient, giving orders to your puppy and not making polite requests, remaining consistent even under duress and sorting problems as they have arisen you should now have a well-trained dog who is welcomed everywhere and who will give you years of loyalty, fun and enjoyment.

Finally, at the end of his life the last thing you can do for your dog is to recognise when he has had enough. His loyal loving eyes will tell you when the time has come. Do not be selfish, be generous and kind and let him go.

INDEX

Also published by Merlin Unwin Books

The Byerley Turk Jeremy James

Advice from a Gamekeeper John Cowan

The BASC Gameshooter's Pocket Guide Michael Brook

Mushrooming with Confidence Alexander Schwab

The Countryman's Bedside Book by BB

Hedgerow Medicine J & M Bruton-Seal

A Shropshire Lad A.E. Housman

The Hare Jill Mason

for our full list of books see
www.merlinunwin.co.uk

FIONA BAIRD grew up in the Ashdown Forest in Sussex surrounded by well-behaved Golden Retrievers which had been bred and gundog-trained by her mother. Fiona later trained her own first bitch (Killie) to become a successful competitor in field trials and has continued breeding and training professionally ever since.

Using her successful no-nonsense methods she has now trained over 25 different breeds from Beaucerons to Lhasa Apsos, mostly in basic discipline. She has also trained a large number of gundogs.

Today, she gives one-to-one lessons in training as well as assistance in correcting bad habits.